How to Become a
Professional Baseball Player

How to Become a Professional Baseball Player

by Bo Durkac

McFarland & Company, Inc., Publishers
Jefferson, North Carolina, and London

Library of Congress Cataloguing-in-Publication Data

Durkac, Bo, 1972–
    How to become a professional baseball player
/ by Bo Durkac.
        p.   cm.
    Includes index.

    ISBN-13: 978-0-7864-1587-8
    softcover : 50# alkaline paper ∞

    1. Baseball — Handbooks, manuals, etc.   2. Baseball players —
Handbooks, manuals, etc.   I. Title.
GV867.3.D87   2003
796.357'02 — dc21   2003003638

British Library cataloguing data are available

Cover photograph: ©2003 Corbis Images

Manufactured in the United States of America

McFarland & Company, Inc., Publishers
  Box 611, Jefferson, North Carolina 28640
    www.mcfarlandpub.com

Table of Contents

To Lance and Brandi.
Thanks for putting up with your big brother.

Introduction

Although the title may suggest differently, "How to Become a Professional Baseball Player" is not as simple as "How to Retile Your Kitchen Floor" or "Replacing a Blown Head Gasket: Eight Simple Steps." When you are down on your hands and knees carefully sliding each piece of tile together, no one is knocking the trowel out of your hand. Same thing in the garage. No one is taking your impact wrench away from you — unless, of course, you just ticked off your wife. Furthermore, I can't say, "If you do this, this, and this and avoid that, that, and that, you'll play pro baseball someday." Professional sports is the only occupation I know in which someone is actively trying to prevent you from doing your job, and because of its nature, there is a talent, or lack of talent, factor involved. Talent, however, isn't the only force working against you.

The road to professional baseball is beset on all sides by a host of temptations and frustrations. Many a gifted ballplayer has seen his road to superstardom cut short by drugs, women, or the bane of all the blue-collar athletes of the world, apathy. Oftentimes, the key to making it is simply maintaining your focus. For example, I have a theory that when every college baseball player begins his career, he has professional aspirations. There comes a point in his career, however, when he comes to the crossroads, and these are the options:

(1) He knows he has the ability to play professionally (either scouts or his coaches tell him so), and he puts forth maximum effort to achieve that goal. He becomes a pro — and a usually a good one.

(2) He has the ability but lacks the desire to pursue it with the intensity it requires. Perhaps he met a girl or found his niche academically and decided that the long, winding, tortuous road of professional baseball is just not worth it. (My father had a similar situation upon

finishing his collegiate basketball career at Cornell University in 1967 back when the Ivy League was one of the better leagues in the country. He could have played professionally in Europe, but he was more interested in finishing veterinary school, marrying my mother, and starting a family — all three of which he did. Although I could not imagine ending my baseball career with my last college game, he never felt the pangs of regret for doing so, and I kid him about that all the time.)

(3) He has busted his tail and tasted some success at the collegiate level, but with limited ability, the scouts don't think too highly of him. Regardless, he will continue to work hard to reach his goal (i.e., my experience).

(4) He has virtually no chance of playing past college, and he knows it, so he is content just being part of the team.

College baseball will undoubtedly be part of your baseball future. Which road will you choose?

My mission with this book is to help you reach the minor leagues. No one ever said it will be easy, but what in life worth having is easy? I will help you make the right choices and avoid the pitfalls that I — or teammates of mine — have experienced. You must understand that all I can do is point you in the right direction; from there, it's all about how badly you want it. Personally, I wanted to be a professional baseball player almost as badly as I wanted my next breath of air. Fortunately, I was able to achieve my goal. I have traveled the path, and I have loved every minute of it. For the rest of my life, I will always be able to say that I was a professional baseball player. That's a heckuva nice feeling.

Throughout this book, I will use different baseball terms, and for further help in understanding these words and phrases, I have included a glossary. As the consummate student of the game, I have avidly followed baseball on television and in the print media for my entire life. During every interview or story that I'd come across, I'd always seem to hear the term "mental," as in "mentally tough" or how baseball is a "mental game" more than a physical one. I never quite understood what the ballplayer meant by that until I actually played pro ball. To me, the term "mental" or "smart" means this: Once you get to a certain level of play — say, the big leagues — the talent factor becomes less of an issue than at the lower levels because in the "Bigs," everyone is talented. Oh, sure, guys like Alex Rodriguez and Omar Vizquel and Randy Johnson are hugely talented, but they are the exceptions. The vast majority of big leaguers are not supremely faster or stronger or harder-throwing than their AA counterparts; they just have their individual skills honed a little bit better and are a little more consistent.

Look, don't worry if you can't run the 60-yard-dash in 6.5 seconds or throw 95 MPH or hit the ball 450 feet. Most big leaguers, believe it or not, can't do those things, either. I'll mention later in the book about how a pitcher has to master his release point for an inside corner fastball with two strikes and how a hitter has to have his swing so finely tuned that when he gets the pitch he wants, he can hammer it. The physical part — the fine-tuning — must come first. Once you've attained that ability to duplicate the same action over and over again, then the mental part becomes a bigger factor in your success. The ability to do these routine tasks — to field the routine groundball every time, to spot your fastball and to throw a breaking pitch for a strike, and to hit the fastball when it's thrown over the heart of the plate — is what ultimately separates the major leaguer from the minor leaguer.

Finally, most "How To" books are not written in the first-person voice. Bob Vila would rarely, if ever, say, "What I like to do next is to take out my trowel" or "I once worked on a house." In that regard, this book is different. I want you to remember who is doing the writing. I am simply a small-town farm boy with minimal athletic ability who played seven years of professional baseball — including play on three other continents, mind you. Yes, it was definitely the "low" minors, but I was paid, and at least I had a chance of reaching the big leagues.

Throughout this book, whenever I assess my talent, I am not being self-deprecating, just honest: if you took the natural ability of every baseball player in organized, affiliated minor league baseball over the last twenty-five years, my natural ability would probably rank in the bottom 10 percent. The sad part for me is that most of my former teammates and opponents would undoubtedly agree with my assessment. Fortunately, baseball is a sport that will reward you for hard work and dedication. Unlike football and basketball, sports in which you can be restricted by a sheer lack of height, speed, or size, you do not need to be a superhuman athlete to succeed at baseball.

Furthermore, a good friend of mine constantly tells me that I went further with less talent than anyone he's ever seen. Such a statement can be taken one of two ways: I had no athletic ability or I did a lot with what I've been given. I opt for the latter inference. Certainly, I could curse my mother and father for their lousy genetics, but let's be reasonable. For the rest of my life, I can look in the mirror and say that I gave myself every possible chance to succeed. I didn't throw my career away on drugs or alcohol or women or a bad attitude. I played a lot longer than other, more talented players, and in that, I can take solace. Yes, I had a little bit of talent, but most of my limited success is due to desire — desire to learn, desire to improve, and desire to be as good as I could possibly be.

Therefore, whenever I refer to myself throughout the book, I want you to think of yourself. Trust me: from a talent standpoint I was unbelievably average. There is no reason why you cannot someday receive a paycheck to play baseball. Perhaps you will not, but if you take care of everything you can control, at least you will have given yourself a chance to succeed. You will never have to look in the mirror and wonder, "What if?" I can't imagine having to carry around *that* burden for the rest of my life.

Prologue

When I was fourteen, I found my father so ignorant that I
could barely stand to be around him. By the time I was twenty-
one, I was amazed at how much he learned in seven years.
— Mark Twain

When I was in high school in the late 1980s and early 1990s, the
thought of my reading a book like the one you are now reading would
have been preposterous. You see, I was one of the top athletes in the
north Pittsburgh area, and it wasn't a question of if I would play college sports but rather which sport. For example, during my senior year
of high school, I was first team All-Conference quarterback, All-Pitts-
burgh Area in hockey, and one the top baseball players in all of Western PA. While the hockey offers never really came in — traditionally,
Western PA is not exactly a hotbed of hockey talent — I could have played
football and baseball at just about every small college in Western PA. I
didn't need some seven-year minor leaguer telling me how to make
myself into a pro baseball player.

Ah, but how times change. I went from being a cocky 18-year-old
to a humbled 28-year-old. Baseball can do that to you. During my first
foray into organized minor league baseball, as a 23-year-old playing for
the Visalia Oaks of the California League, I was amazed at the talent level
around me. It didn't take long for me to realize that I would make more
money in baseball by using my brain than by using my body. When I
saw the supremely talented likes of Miguel Tejada, Ben Grieve, Russ
Ortiz, Gary Matthews, Jr., and Ben Davis (just to name a few), I knew
that my path to the big leagues would be about as smooth as the surface of Mars.

Like every other obstacle I faced during my ten-year search for
baseball Valhalla — lack of footspeed and raw homerun power, having

to transfer colleges after my freshman year, not having the Arizona Diamondbacks invest any money in me (I'll explain that later)—I used it as motivation to fuel the flames of my own personal desire. Unfortunately, all the desire in the world doesn't mean a whole lot unless there is a certain amount of talent to accompany it. In the latter category, I came up short. But I didn't know or care what I lacked; I was hell-bent on using what I *did* have.

It's funny, but when I tell people how comparatively under-talented I was, they don't believe me. They figure if I played minor league baseball for seven years that I had to have a lot of ability, but that was simply not the case. Perhaps compared to a local junior college player I am more talented, but in the big picture, it's not true. As a position player in baseball, your natural ability is rated by the following five "tools": hitting for average, hitting for power, running speed, fielding, and throwing. I have always been both unfailingly objective and keenly aware—traits unbelievably rare in most ballplayers—of my talents; it's an athlete's nature to think he is better than what he really is. I would have ranked my "tools" like this: above average, below average, poor, average, average, respectively. Yes, some baseball people may think otherwise in certain categories, but I think these assessments are pretty accurate. It's no secret that my natural ability to play baseball was very average compared to most professional players, and I had to bust my tail just to get to play seven years in the low minors.

The purpose of this book is to give you every chance to succeed in your pursuit of playing professional baseball. The very fact that you are reading this book tells me two things: you weren't blessed with a ridiculous amount of talent and you are looking for every edge you can get. Notice how I have never asserted to help you reach the major leagues; the ability to do that is based more on your level of innate athleticism. In addition, I never played in the big leagues myself, so implying that I know what it takes to make it would be dishonest. Certainly, it isn't all about natural talent, but having a good deal of it will make your journey to The Show a heckuva lot easier—and shorter. No, I would rather focus on taking care of the little things to give you every opportunity to succeed.

I have always said, "There are so many factors out of your control in the baseball world that, rather than focusing on these things, you should worry about the stuff that you can control." You'll see that this is the recurring theme throughout this book. The first step to reaching the big leagues is reaching the minor leagues. From there, anything can happen.

Perhaps the most well-documented case of coming out of nowhere to become a superstar is Mike Piazza's. If you didn't already know, Piazza is the godson of former Los Angeles Dodger manager Tommy Lasorda, and, as a favor to Piazza's father, Vince, the Dodgers selected Piazza in the 62nd round of the 1988 Free Agent Draft. Historically, a 62nd-rounder has almost a better chance of being struck by lightning than reaching the big leagues, but Piazza took the opportunity and ran with it. All he needed was his foot in the door, and once you get that uniform on, it's all up to you.

Along these lines, most marginal professional baseball players say that the greatest amount of pressure they faced in their careers centered on their being drafted. I agree wholeheartedly. In Chapter 14, I'll present the odds of going from amateur baseball to professional baseball and from the minor leagues to the major leagues, and the odds are roughly one in one hundred versus one in eight, respectively. Once you sign a minor league contract, anything can happen. Again, the bonus babies of the world will get every chance to succeed whereas one bad half-season may earn you your release. That's the unfair nature of the beast, but it has always been that way. Deal with it. If life isn't fair, then baseball is horribly biased. But you can't do anything without a uniform on your back. My goal is to put that uniform on your back.

This book is one part instructional, one part informational, and one part motivational. To be sure, books about hitting and pitching a baseball, life in the minor leagues, and how to become a success have already been written, but to my knowledge, they have never been combined into one work. I mention later in the hitting chapter that I could speak and write for hours about the finer points of hitting a baseball. The same holds true for all other parts of baseball — and from an information and motivation standpoint as well. Rather than going into great depth with each phase of baseball and life, I chose simply to touch on them. Understand that there are no secrets to becoming a pro baseball player; you need to have sufficient amounts of instruction, information, and motivation. I will attempt to give you enough of each of these to get you started, and I trust you to do the rest yourself. But know this: it can be done. How badly do you want it?

1

Pitching

When the late Ted Williams took over as the manager of the Washington Senators in 1968, he told his hitters "you have to understand pitching if you're ever going to understand hitting." Williams was obviously one outstanding hitter, and believe me, he understood pitching. He was known for his ability to "think along with the pitcher" and to "guess," and his career statistics speak for themselves. Even though I'm no Ted Williams, I feel I can also speak ably as to what makes a good pitcher.

I'm not going to sit here and give you a lot of theory about pitching mechanics, as I hated when pitchers tried to talk about hitting theory with me. The two skills are as different — at least physically — as apples and oranges. The reason, though, that I feel reasonably qualified to speak about pitching is because I faced enough good pitching in my career to know what separates the good pitchers from the poor ones. The point of this chapter is to give you the basics of pitching.

The importance of mechanics

I have always been a "student of the game," and more specifically, a student of hitting. Part of plying my trade as a hitter is trying to figure out how pitchers pitch. When I talk to pitchers about pitching, mechanics seems to be one of the most important facets of becoming a quality pitcher.

During the 2000 season, I discussed a certain pitcher on our Chico Heat team with one of the best hurlers I have ever faced, former AAA pitcher Randy Phillips. (In one of those unfair twists of fate, Phillips sustained a minor arm injury just days before he was to be called up to the big leagues, and he never received a second chance.) The pitcher in question, who had put up some pretty good numbers at the AA level, was really struggling with his control, and I asked Randy what he thought. Without hesitation, Randy said it was because the pitcher had lousy mechanics. Phillips, on the other hand, had textbook mechanics. In fact, after joining the Sonoma County Crushers in the spring of 2001, I asked teammate and pitcher Brian Grant if he had played with Phillips during his days with the Toronto Blue Jays organization. Well, not only did he say that he did, but he also said that all the other pitchers would stop and gather around to watch Phillips throw in his bullpen workouts. He was that good. Personally, I can confirm that Phillips was that good, having faced him numerous times in 1999. I mean, he never threw a fastball over the middle twelve inches of the plate, and as a hitter, I made my living off fastballs over those twelve inches. Every strike from him was a fastball on the corner, a big curveball, or a perfectly thrown changeup. Phillips was not Pedro Martinez–dirty or Randy Johnson–intimidating; he was Greg Maddux–frustrating. In fact, because of his mound presence, his mechanics, and the command of his pitches, we started to call him "Maddux."

The reason I bring up Phillips is to illustrate the importance of good mechanics. Certainly, good mechanics can't guarantee success, just as a fluid stroke does not guarantee success as a hitter, but at least you have a fighting chance. Also, when a pitcher with good mechanics struggles, the problem is usually a little bit easier for a pitching coach to pinpoint. If, on the other hand, the pitcher has lousy mechanics, detecting and fixing the flaw becomes much more difficult.

Along these lines, another good pitcher with whom I played, a guy with a "cup of coffee" in the major leagues, felt that the key to pitching is "the ability to duplicate the same mechanics." By that, he means that as a pitcher, you have to be able to repeat the exact same motion and exact same release point for every pitch you throw: fastball in, fastball away, curveball, slider, changeup. Just as I cannot tell you how to hit a line drive, I cannot tell you how to throw a fastball on the black; you must learn for yourself. But I know one thing: it all starts with good mechanics.

The K.I.S.S. theory (keep it simple, stupid)

Certainly, one of the easiest ways to ensure good mechanics—whether pitching or hitting—is to keep everything as simple as possible. If you watch a big league game, you'll see that most pitchers, when pitching from the windup, no longer bring their hands over their heads. The reason is that it's basically a wasted movement and has little or no

Bringing the hands overhead in the windup.

Bringing the hands to the chest in the windup.

bearing on the pitcher's velocity. Beyond that phase of the delivery, I have no other recommendations, and everything else should be based on personal preference. The only other thing I would say is to avoid the extremes. By that, I mean avoid a high, Juan Marichal–like leg kick or excessive stride length.

Now, you're probably thinking, "Wow, Bo, if mechanics is all it takes, then why can't more guys spot their fastballs like the Madduxes of the world?" Well, like any skill in sports—shooting a basketball or throwing a football or putting a golf ball—certain athletes simply have a gift to perform these feats. Even more frustrating is the fact that many of these athletes don't look the part. What I mean is that guys like Greg Maddux and Joe Montana look more like the guys who would do your taxes than guys going to the Hall of Fame. I have no explanation why they became so good at their crafts; they just are. Is it excessive practice? Heck, lots of guys put in hours upon hours honing their skills. Is it good technique? Lots of guys have great mechanics. The bottom line is that guys like Maddux and Montana have "it," and the rest of us mortals don't. But fear not. You may not be going to the Hall of fame, but that doesn't mean you can't enjoy a successful athletic career.

Another big reason that mechanics are so important is perception. As you progress in this game, you will see that a college coach's or pro scout's perception of your ability is oftentimes more important than your actual ability. A pitcher with a smooth, effortless windup is generally looked at more favorably than a pitcher with a choppy, flawed windup. For starters, a pitcher with a fluid delivery is less apt to experience arm troubles, and in this day and age, with fragile arms and even more fragile psyches, a pitcher's durability is as hot a commodity as his fastball. Secondly, if a coach or scout is evaluating two pitchers of equal "stuff," he will usually opt for the one with the smooth delivery. He knows that the choppy pitcher will need much more fine-tuning to maximize his ability, and changing a pitcher's mechanics leads to changing his arm slot. Once a pitcher is forced to learn a new arm slot, he will require scores and scores of innings to burn it into his muscle memory. Most coaches and scouts don't want to wait that long to see if a kid can develop into a quality pitcher.

Now, don't tell me that a pitcher's windup—like a hitter's swing—is natural and unchangeable. As a pitcher, you set the pace. You can windup whenever you want, at whatever speed you want. Unlike hitting, there are no variables. Your job is to provide the variables to the hitter, and you can do so of your own volition. Need an example of someone who "changed" his windup? How about Pat Ahearne? He grew up in California when Orel Hershiser of the Los Angeles Dodgers was in his heyday. Ahearn, who went on to win a national championship in 1992 at Pepperdine University, decided to pattern his windup after Hershiser's. You would be utterly amazed at how similar the pitchers' windups are, and Ahearne eventually received a cup of coffee in the big leagues. You don't have to copy a specific pitcher's windup; just practice a fluid windup over and over again until it's second nature. Again, how bad do you want to be good?

The Two Fatal Flaws

In regards to mechanics, I once heard a pitching coach say, "There are really only two things a pitcher can do to mess himself up: rush himself and not get his arm up." When I was with the Diamondbacks, the pitchers would go through their daily "stick drill" routine, in which they would simulate their pitching motions but use a stick rather than a baseball for proper arm action. Naturally, I had to ask our minor league pitching coordinator, and former New York Yankees pitching coach, Mark Connor, what the purpose was. He replied that there were two reasons: 1) to ensure that the pitchers found their balance points and 2) to get their arms into their proper slots — basically, the same key points that I heard the other pitching coach say. Also, and on a lesser scale, the throwing motion involving a stick is a lot less taxing on the arm than is a baseball.

The balance point is that moment in the delivery when the pitcher has rocked back and kicked up his leg but before he starts his motion towards the plate. Generally, when a pitcher "rushes," he starts his motion to the plate before he has gathered himself at the balance point. Now, the natural flow of his delivery has been disrupted, and his arm slot — the most important part of a pitcher's delivery — bears the brunt, making it nearly impossible to spot his fastball. The best way to make sure you are finding your balance point is to stand at the balance point for five or ten seconds before beginning your motion to the plate. Until you can hold this position successfully in practice, it is unlike that you'll be able to so in a game situation.

"Not getting the arm up" is often a result of rushing, but it can also be a problem in its own right. When a pitcher fails to elevate his arm to get on top of the ball (as opposed to the less-desired behind the ball), he cannot throw the ball on a downward plane. Any pitcher at any level

The balance point: all pitchers must find this point in the delivery.

A front view of the balance point.

A side view of failing to get the arm up.

A side view of properly getting the arm up.

of play knows that making mistakes up in the strike zone usually means doom. Oftentimes, "throwing up" (a common rag from a bench full of hecklers is "Someone call the doctor—he's throwing up") is a result of fatigue, but failing to get his arm up and his hand on top of the ball can bring about the same problem.

One thing that will help you get your arm up is proper separation of the ball from the glove. Some pitchers who struggle with getting their arms up have to exaggerate by taking the throwing hand out of the glove exceptionally early. (To me, it's the same as a hitter who fails to get his

Successfully getting hand on top of the ball.

front foot down on time. Because doing so is hugely important, if he needs to get it down almost uncomfortably early, then he must.) Also, when removing the ball from the glove, both the glove hand and the throwing hand must separate in a "thumbs-down" position. In other words, as the separation process begins, the thumbs should be the fingers that are the closest to the ground. If not, then you would be "cupping" the ball, and it would be more difficult to get on top of the ball.

Finally, I once heard a pitching coach discuss the importance of using both arms to pitch. He said that when you walk, you don't swing

Failure to get hand on top of the ball.

just one arm. The same is true when running. If you ran with one arm pumping and one arm down at your side, not only would you not run as fast, but you would also look pretty silly as well. He said that pitching is no different and that pulling back with the glove-arm elbow is as important as thrusting forward with the throwing arm. You must use the leverage of the glove-arm to create that little bit of extra torque to add a little bit more life to your fastball. I agree.

Controlling what you can control

The theme of this book is that there are enough parts of your game — and your life — that you cannot change, so it is imperative to control those parts that you can. And, yes, I will continue to harp on this theme throughout this book. One of the things that, for the most part, you cannot control is the velocity of your fastball. You can't do anything about the fact that you can't throw the ball 98 MPH, but over the course of my many years of baseball, one thing I never understood is how some left-handed pitchers don't have good pickoff moves.

Having a good pickoff move requires zero talent. None. All it takes is the desire to develop one. Two of the best pickoff moves of the 1990s belonged to Terry Mulholland and Andy Pettitte. While both of these men have enjoyed long and productive careers, neither of them has what would be considered outstanding stuff. One thing is for certain, though: their lifetime ERA's have been lowered by their abilities not only to pick off runners but also to keep runners close to first base. Think about the number of times Mulholland's defense was able to turn a double play when it might not have been if the runner at first could have gotten a larger lead. Or perhaps the number of times a runner was unable to go from first base to third base on Pettitte because of the runner's abbreviated lead.

If a lefty should have a good pickoff move, then all pitchers should be able to incorporate a "slide-step" in their deliveries. With the track meet that took place in the major leagues in the 1980s, pitchers began to search for a way to keep baserunners from stealing so easily, and the slide-step became weapon of choice. Basically, when pitching from the stretch, a pitcher will "slide" his lead foot towards home plate rather than kicking it high as he would in the windup. The upside to the slide-step is that a pitcher will deliver the ball more quickly to the plate and therefore help control the running game. The downside, though, is that he is now rushing himself, something pitchers try to avoid.

I have asked several pitching coaches about the slide-step, and most of them don't like it. They say that most pitchers are unable to find their proper release points consistently when using the slide-step, and the result is a loss of control. One of the pitching coaches actually said, "I'd rather have a runner on second after stealing a base while making quality pitches than give up a double and allow that runner to score from first." Since most pitchers struggle with using the slide-step and most pitching coaches discourage it, wouldn't it make sense to learn how to use it before they take it away from you? Once again, it comes down to a matter of desire and how badly you want to integrate it. There is no substitute for repetition in baseball, and learning the slide-step is no different.

Pitching styles

Generally, there two styles of pitchers: "tall and fall" and "drop and drive." Which type of pitcher you become is based predominately on your body type. The "tall and fall" pitcher is someone who uses his height, the long reach which typically accompanies that height, and leverage to generate his fastball. In today's game, the classic example of this type of pitcher is Randy Johnson. At 6'10" tall, he uses his height 1) to throw the ball upwards of 100 MPH and 2) to throw a ball that is constantly traveling on a downward plane. The combination of these two factors makes The Big Unit one of the most dominating pitchers of this generation.

To me, the best example of a "drop and drive" pitcher is Tom Seaver. Although he retired almost twenty years ago, baseball fans of his era will undoubtedly remember him as having a dirt stain on his uniform pants where his right knee came in contact with the ground during each pitch. Seaver used his powerful legs to propel his pitches to home plate, and in doing so he became one of the dominant pitchers of *his* generation.

Of course, if you can combine these two styles into one, your chances of becoming a great pitcher increase. If you look at Roger Clemens, I think you'll see both styles at work. Clemens stands 6'4" tall, but he weighs about 225 lbs. A fitness freak of historical proportions, he employs the lethal combination of his massive legs and thick torso to complement the downward plane that comes from being so tall. Again, I use these three pitchers as examples for their styles, not their talents. All three of these men are first ballot Hall of Famers, and what they have accomplished in their careers is more a testament to what they were blessed with physically than anything else. You can't expect to duplicate these pitchers' talents; you can, however, duplicate their work ethic and their mechanics.

The different pitches

> There are three things that can a pitch can have: velocity, movement, and location. If you have two of these three, you'll win. If you have all three, you're unbeatable. — Tom Seaver

Now, let's talk about pitch selection. Assuming you haven't been blessed with a 90+ MPH fastball, you'll need to develop the ability to spot your fastball (throw it on the inner and outer two-and-a-half inches of the plate) and one or more offspeed pitches for a strike. As for the fastball, there are the two-seam and four-seam varieties. Take a baseball, look at it, and see where the seams (technically, there is only one seam) come together and almost touch. If you place your first and second fingers either upon those two seams or across them perpendicularly, then you have the two-seam grip. For the four-seamer, rotate the baseball so that the horseshoe is facing either directly right or directly left. If you grip the baseball so that your first and second fingers are perpendicular to those seams, then you have the four-seam grip. Now, imagine releasing the ball from your hand, and envision the four seams rotating in the same direction, thus the name.

The two-seam fastball grip.

The two-seam fastball is designed to create movement on the pitch. A few years ago, I heard Bobby Cox, manager of the Atlanta Braves, say that the toughest pitch in baseball to hit is the moving fastball, and I have to agree. However, let me qualify that statement just a bit: it is the toughest pitch to hit hard. Making contact with a late-moving fastball normally results in a broken bat (whereas trying to hit a properly thrown changeup, the other pitch often regarded as the best in baseball, usually means a swing and a miss). Some pitchers are able to get that little bit of late movement, and others aren't. For example, Greg Maddux gets all his movement by exerting pressure on the ball with his fingers, but if it were that simple, every pitcher would be able to make the ball dance like that. All I can say about that is to experiment with different grips and pressures to determine what works best for you.

The four-seam fastball, on the other hand, is designed to travel as straight as possible, which is why infielders use that same grip in throwing the ball across the infield. A pitcher uses a four-seam grip either when he wants either to paint a corner or to throw the ball right down the middle of the plate.

The curveball, for nearly a century the second pitch of choice of most major league pitchers, has all but disappeared from today's game due to both the added stress it creates on the arm and the vertical shrinking of the strike zone. Three of the most dominating pitchers of the last forty years—Sandy Koufax, Dwight Gooden, and Nolan Ryan— featured outstanding curveballs that complemented their blazing fastballs, and the two go hand-in-hand. You see, when a pitcher uncorks a 95 MPH fastball that travels to the

The four-seam fastball grip.

upper edge of the strike zone and then follows it with a curveball that starts out like that fastball only to "fall off the table," well, then you have a Hall of Fame-caliber pitcher. In today's game, though, the high strike has virtually disappeared, rendering the high heater and subsequently, the big curveball, basically useless. Therefore, the vast majority of pitchers today use the slider as their breaking pitch.

The slider came into being in the 1960s, and no less a hitter than the great Hank Aaron said it was the toughest pitch to hit. The pitch is designed to look like a fastball for the first 30 or so feet of the pitch, only to break suddenly and sharply out of the strike zone. The slider is simply a harder, tighter version of the curveball, and it can be gripped in one of two ways. First, you can grip it like the curveball and snap your wrist across your body to get the two-plane movement that is the most effective (two-plane means that rather than breaking directly horizontally or directly vertically, it breaks both down and to the left or right). Or, you can throw a "cut" fastball, in which you place your first and second fingers together and grip the ball slightly off-center to the outside part. Then, the throw the ball as normal, and the pressure of your two fingers in that spot can cause the ball to break sharply to the left (if

The slider grip.

you're right-handed). Mariano Rivera of the New York Yankees became one of the best closers in baseball — and the best postseason pitcher in baseball history — with a "cutter" thrown upwards of 95 MPH. Again, the grip/ pressure thing is not a guarantee of success; you'll have to determine what works best for you.

Finally, the changeup, when thrown properly, can be as difficult as any pitch to hit, and the reason is this: it looks like a fastball at the release point, but by the time the hitter's eyes recognize that it's not, it's too late. I have seen several different ways to grip the changeup, and again, it's all based on personal preference and feel. For example, Tom Glavine was simply a big league pitcher until one day, he picked up a ball in the outfield during batting practice. He gripped it in an

A front view of a circle-changeup.

unusual way and threw it to a teammate. By accident, he found a new grip for a baffling changeup that turned him into a potential Hall of Famer.

The important thing is that the changeup must be thrown with the same arm speed as the fastball. In other words, the arm must travel at the same speed as when throwing the fastball, and the way you grip the ball will determine the actual velocity of the pitch. If you slow down your body or your arm speed on the changeup, good hitters will detect

A side view of a different circle-changeup.

it and murder the offering. Everything must be exactly the same except for the speed of the pitch.

Incidentally, I intentionally omitted the split-fingered fastball, the forkball, the screwball, and the knuckleball because these are advanced pitches for advanced pitchers. If you, as an amateur, can master the fastball, slider, and changeup, you won't need any others pitches to succeed. Throwing more pitches does not automatically make you a better pitcher. Choose quality over quantity.

Some final thoughts

> Hitting is timing; pitching is upsetting timing. — Orel Hershiser

> Don't worry if the .300 hitters hit you; they'll hit your best stuff from time to time. But you can't give up hits to them fellers who can't hit. — Dizzy Dean

The thought process involved in becoming a good pitcher is every bit as important as the physical, i.e., know your hitter. I realize that as an amateur, you generally don't have access to detailed scouting reports as the pros do, but there is one universal truth to pitching: hard stuff in, soft stuff away. Tim Torricelli, my manager in Visalia in 1996, told me something that I never forgot. He played with sluggers Greg Vaughn and Gary Sheffield in the minors, and he said, "You don't get good hitters out pitching up/down or in/out; you get them back to front." What he meant was that to get the good ones out, you have to disrupt their timing.

Think of the strike zone not as a rectangle but as a three-dimensional cube. As a hitter, I want to be quick when hitting the inside fastball, and I want to let the ball travel a little bit farther when hitting the off-speed pitch on the outside part of the plate. I want you to imagine viewing a hitter from directly above home plate, and imagine the ideal position and location of his bat on the inside-corner fastball and the outside-corner off-speed pitch. Got it? Now, the key to pitching is to make the hitter make contact with the inside-corner fastball about 6–8 inches behind where he would like to and with the outside-corner offspeed pitch about 6–8 inches in front of where he'd like to. For the record, most hitters want to make contact with the inside-corner fastball roughly 4–8 inches in front of the front foot (after the stride has taken place) and with the outside-corner offspeed pitch roughly even with the front knee (again, after the stride). If you can consistently do that, then you are disrupting his timing, and in essence, you are pitching.

Obviously, it's not always that simple. There will be times when you'll throw a seemingly perfect pitch and a great hitter will destroy it. There will also be times when you hang a curveball and a great hitter will foul it off. Whenever I work with a young kid on his hitting, the first thing I always do is give him a brief dissertation on how hard hitting is. The same is true for pitching. It's almost paradoxical: if hitting is the toughest thing to do in sports, then stopping hitting should be a pretty easy task, right? Wrong. Both skills are hard to learn and even harder to master. The important thing is to put yourself into the best position possible to succeed, and having good mechanics and a solid mental approach are two of the best ways to help you.

If you flip ahead in the book, there is a part in the hitting section that deals with two-strike hitting. To paraphrase, most good hitters, with two strikes, look for the ball on the outer half of the plate and try to "fight off" the inside fastball. The reason a good hitter looks for the ball away is it forces him to let the ball travel as long as possible before swinging at it. The longer a hitter can watch the ball before swinging at it, the less chance he will be fooled by the pitch. Now, knowing this, and knowing that most good hitters look for the ball away with two strikes, what appears to be the best pitch to throw in a two-strike count? Exactly: a fastball on the inside corner.

Also in the hitting section, I talk about the importance about "grooving" your swing. It does no good whatsoever to work the count into your favor (usually a 2–0 or 3–1 count — fastball counts), get the pitch you want, and then foul it off or hit it weakly. The same is true in pitching. It is of no benefit for a pitcher to get the count to 2–2, get the hitter looking away, and try to hit the inside corner with strike three but instead leave the ball over the heart of the plate where he can hammer it. That's why it's so imperative to be able to spot your fastball, and the only way to do that is to practice and practice and practice.

I realize that you, as a young pitcher, maybe looking for more concrete answers to your questions about pitching than what I have mentioned in this chapter, and that is totally understandable. Heck, when I was 17 and 18 years old, my desire to become a great hitter resulted in my constantly changing my swing in accordance to the latest "theory" I had heard or read about. Looking back, I was willing to do anything to become great, and that's not necessarily a bad thing. I just wish I could have found what worked for me as a 26-year-old back then. Unfortunately, I didn't have the luxury of the top-flight instruction that I would later receive in the professional ranks. My point is that I, or anyone else, can talk pitching theory with you until we're both blue in the face, but theory alone will not turn you into a great pitcher. You need the mechanics, the practice, and the determination to make yourself great. There are no secrets or shortcuts. Get a catcher, a baseball and figure it out for yourself. You know you can do it.

2

Fielding

Dave Concepción, shortstop for Cincinnati's Big Red Machine of the 1970s, once said, "The ability to play a big league shortstop is something you're born with," and I would have to agree. Playing a big league shortstop requires a delicate combination of quick feet, agility, soft hands, and arm strength — four traits that rarely exist in one human being. At the other infield positions, if you're lacking one of these components, you can still become a quality defensive player. For example, if you have good feet and quick hands, you don't need an outstanding arm to play second base. At third base, a strong arm is more important than quick feet. While hitting is much more difficult to improve, becoming a good defensive infielder doesn't require much more than a lot of practice (that's up to you) and good technique (that's up to me).

The importance of becoming a good defensive infielder

In this chapter, I want to talk about infield defense and how important it was to me in allowing me to keep playing professional baseball. Let me start you with a story. In 1998, I joined the Chico Heat, and we had a very powerful offensive club. Normally, the best hitters on a team are the third baseman, the first baseman, the right fielder, and the left fielder. We, however, had a shortstop who was among the league leaders in homeruns, a second baseman who was in the Top 10 in the league in hitting, and a center fielder who hit for both average and power. Therefore, there wasn't much pressure on me to be a walloping hitter, which was good because a walloping hitter I definitely was not. For that year, I hit .263 and drove in only 41 runs in 90 games. I found out the next season that there was a point early in the year that our manager,

Bill Plummer, was entertaining thoughts of releasing me, but because I was playing superb defense and he recognized the importance of that to our team, he kept me around. About three-quarters of the way through the year, Plummer and I began to work diligently on my hitting, and by the end of the regular season, I was starting to get some positive results, even if it was only in batting practice. I was very much looking forward to the following year, looking forward to resuming those lessons that Plummer and I did together. The following year I had the best season of my professional career: I hit .337 with 77 RBI's in 90 games. That is a marked improvement from the previous year, wouldn't you say? The point I'm trying to make, though, is that had my defense not been as good as it was, I might never have received the chance to improve my hitting as I did. Had my hitting not improved, I might not be writing this right now.

I've always had a certain self-awareness about my abilities. Many baseball players are blind to their own weaknesses; I, however, was always keenly aware of mine, and I sought to improve them on a daily basis. For example, when I got to college after having played the middle infield for my entire high school career, my college coach put me at third base. It didn't take a genius to see that with my body type and my lack of foot quickness, I was no longer able to play the middle infield anymore. Furthermore, with my lack of foot speed and lack of outstanding arm strength, I knew I would never be able to play the outfield either. It was during that freshman year that finally decided that I better become a good defensive third baseman, or I might never play an inning of professional baseball my entire life.

You know, everybody today — heck, even eleven years ago, when I was a freshman in college — wants to work on hitting, hitting, and more hitting. For whatever reason, I guess due to my work ethic, I took it upon myself to become a good defensive third baseman, perhaps subconsciously realizing that I would never have the thundering bat that the typical third baseman has. I would say over my college career that I spent an equal amount of time hitting and fielding, and I don't feel that too many players can say that. I worked on everything: backhands, forehands, slow rollers, and the barehanded plays. I was determined to become the best defensive third baseman I could possibly be.

Now, I've already explained that I have been a third baseman, and basically nothing but a third baseman, for my entire professional career, but fielding is fielding, so to speak. In other words, a shortstop or second baseman would say the exact same things that I say if he were writing this chapter. If you watch a major league infielder and compare him to every other major league infielder, you'll see basically the same technique. It's not like hitting, where every player tends to have his own style. Some guys hold the bat high. Some guys hold the bat low. Some guys have a leg kick. Some guys have no stride at all. Some guys pull everything. Some guys hit everything the other way. The bottom line is that they hit, or else they wouldn't be at the big league level. Fielding technique, however, is pretty much universal.

Proper technique: it's all about footwork

In my opinion, too many coaches place a heavy emphasis on soft hands and arm strength when evaluating an infielder's ability. While those two traits are indeed important, I've always felt that the key to becoming a successful defensive infielder is proper footwork. There's a difference between having quick feet and having good footwork. As a youth, I was always one of the slower-footed guys on any team I played on. Believe me, I tried everything: jumping rope, plyometrics, and everything in between. I don't know if any of these drills actually helped me, but I don't think they hurt me. What *did* help me, without a doubt, was the sheer number of ground balls I took over my four years of college. It used to be like pulling teeth sometimes to get coaches or pitchers to hit the extra ground balls I craved, but that's how adamant I was about improving. The only way you learn to handle the myriad tricky hops that are involved in playing third base is actually to have those balls hit to you over and over again. All the plyometrics and jumping rope in the world will not familiarize you with the nuances of playing "the hot corner."

The reason footwork is so important is because of a saying that Jay Phillips, our infield coach at Virginia Tech, impressed upon me from the day I set foot on campus: "If you move your feet, you can pick your hop." Let me explain. There are three types of hops that a groundball can take. One is the "big hop," one is the "short hop," and one is the "in-between hop." Footwork is of huge importance because all the arm strength and soft hands in the world won't help you with the "in-between" hop, which I will explain later.

The "big hop" refers to the groundball that may bounce anywhere between four and ten times before it gets to the fielder. Now, with each hop — no matter how big or how small the bounce — there is an apex.

Staying back to field the big hop.

Catching the ball on the "big hop" means catching the ball at or near the apex. If you can position your feet properly to catch the ball at its highest point, you can negate any bad hops. After all, I've never seen a ball hit an air molecule and take a wicked bounce. In other words, once the ball has hit and the ground and bounced up, it will stay on the same path. Also, the ball will be closer to your eyes, enabling you to follow it better.

The "short hop" refers to catching the ball immediately after the ball hits the ground. Yes, "immediately" is a very vague term, so let me use distances as well to give you an idea. On that same four- to ten-hop groundball, you want to catch the ball as close as possible to where it hits the ground, and I think anything farther than eight inches away from you is a bad hop waiting to happen. The reason you want to catch the ball so close to its bounce is to reduce the effects of a bad hop. Think of it logically. Imagine the spot where a ball takes its last hop and travels on a perfect path. Now imagine that same spot but with a bad hop involved. The farther away your glove is from where the ball hit the ground, the greater the deviation from the true hop line. Therefore, if you can catch the ball before it gets a chance to deviate significantly, you can all but nullify the bad hop.

Reaching out with the hands to create a short-hop.

Using a one-handed approach to create a short-hop and to avoid an in-between hop.

Finally, the "in-between hop," the cause of 95 percent of all black eyes and lost teeth on a baseball field, is the hop you want to avoid. Picture a four-hop groundball coming at you. Let's say you are too close to the ball on its fourth hop to catch the "big hop" and too far away from it to catch the "short hop." Now, my friend, you are in "no-man's" land, and you are in trouble. (It's similar to tennis. You either want to be at the baseline or at the net; if you're in the middle, you are dead meat.) When those nasty, top-spin groundballs take a last hop and you are caught "in-between," I don't care if your name is Ozzie Smith or Cal Ripken or Omar Vizquel — you are done. When a sharply struck groundball takes that last, wicked hop, you simply cannot react in time to field the ball cleanly. The only chance you have is to knock it down with your chest (or your face). Wouldn't you rather use your glove instead? That's why you bought it, right? Proper footwork will get you into the proper position to field the "big hop" and the "short hop" and allow you to avoid the dreaded "in-between" hop.

To start, though, I first must emphasize proper fielding technique. Yes, it is difficult for me to explain proper technique without my being

The hop you want to avoid — the in-between hop. Notice how far away I am from the final hop.

there, but one of the best ways to learn is to watch the people who are the best at doing it. To this day, I always mention the fact that I learned almost as much about proper fielding technique by watching Miguel Tejada of the Oakland A's back when I played against him in the California League in 1996 as I did actually having proper technique taught to me. I would recommend that you do the same. There's nothing wrong with videotaping a major league baseball game and watching a major league shortstop fielding a routine ground ball. I will bet the ranch that every major league fielder looks exactly the same, except in respect to body type and arm strength of course.

The Ready Position

When I instruct infield technique to young kids, I start by getting all of them into the "ready position." The "ready position" is my generic term — actually my father used that term when he coached my Little League team, and I have since adopted it — for the body position from which all athletic movements begin. If you look at a hockey goalie or a defensive back in football or a perimeter defender in basketball, they all start from the same basic athletic position: knees slightly bent, weight on the balls of the feet, and head up, and hands *not on the knees*. This is the position you want to be in when the ball is making contact with the bat. If you watch a tennis player preparing to return a serve, you'll notice that he takes a little hop just as the ball is striking his opponent's racket. Not to get too technical, but it is a simple case of overcoming your body's state of inertia. ("A body at rest tends to stay at rest unless acted upon by an outside force. A body in motion tends to stay in motion unless acted upon by an outside force.") When the tennis player takes that little hop, he is taking his body out of a state of rest and putting it into a state of motion, and anybody knows that is easier to move quickly if you are already moving than if your body is at rest.

The Approach

So, contact is made, and the ball is on its way to you. To keep things simple, I am discussing only the routine ground ball, the ground ball that is hit with medium speed directly at you. Now, since your body was in motion with your little hop step, you want to keep your body in motion until the ball is fielded and is on its way to its designated base. This is the tricky part. You want to move to and through the baseball, without committing so much that you cannot handle the bad hop. It is a very tricky line, a very delicate balance. (It's like taking a stride as a hitter;

I can't tell you exactly *when* to do so. Good hitters simply have that innate timing). If you stay back too long, you let the ball play you or you may not throw the ball in time to get the runner at first base. If you charge the ball too quickly, you may not be able to handle a tricky hop on a bad field. That is why I want you to watch a big league infielder field a routine ground ball in a game situation. Ninety-nine times out of a hundred, on a routine groundball, a major league infielder will deliver the ball to first base with just barely enough time to get the runner. The way I like to explain the timing element is this: you do not receive an extra out by throwing a runner out by six steps as opposed to one step. In other words, "Be quick, but never hurry."

Understand that it's not enough simply to catch the ball; you must catch it in a position to deliver a strong and accurate throw to first base. Let me make an analogy that occurs in another of my favorite sports: billiards. I was playing one of my uncles in pool several years ago, and I was shooting very well that day. The key to being a good pool shooter is to make a ball with one shot and have the cue ball go into position for your next shot, and on this day, I was doing exactly that. My uncle then remarked, "You know, Bo, pool is easy when you have easy shot after easy shot." It's not enough just to make a shot; it must lead to an easy, subsequent shot.

Fielding is the same way. Whether you are throwing on the run, going to your backhand, or going to the glove side, you must put yourself into as good a position as possible to make a throw once you've caught the ball. All of this work must be done before the ball gets to you, and thus the importance of proper angles. Baseball people use the term "banana route" to illustrate this point. If you viewed an infielder from directly above him, you would see that when routine groundball is hit to him, he does *not* approach the ball straight at it. Doing so would force his body's momentum towards home plate, as opposed to first base. Instead, his first step will be slightly to the right of the path of the ball, then he will take one or two steps forward, and then he will step slightly to his left as he is fielding the ball. This curved path to the ball is called the "banana route," and all good infielders do it. In doing so, he has used his body's momentum to put more velocity on his throw.

Catching the Ball

At this point the ball has reached you, so now it's time to discuss the proper fielding position. I think the biggest flaw with a young infielder is that he catches the ball underneath his body as opposed to in front of him. The reason you reach out to catch the ball is the same reason you catch fly balls over your head as opposed to the "basket-catch" style: your eyes can follow the ball better. When catching the fly ball over your head, your eyes can track the ball all the way to the glove. In the basket-catch style, though, the three feet or so that the ball travels from over your head to your midsection makes it very difficult for your eyes to follow; the ball is going *past* your eyes rather than *at* your eyes. When fielding a groundball properly, by reaching out in front of your body as opposed to catching the ball beneath you, you've similarly eliminated the last three feet or so of distance that the eyes cannot easily follow.

To get the hands out in front of your body, your arms must be fully extended, with both the head and the butt as close to the ground as possible. One of the keys to getting into this position is spreading your feet well beyond shoulder-width. Once again, I envision watching a young Miguel Tejada fielding ground balls. Granted, he is no taller than 5'9", but I was amazed at how close to the ground he got when he fielded. Also, if I may make a geometrical analogy here, you want your feet to be square, and I'll explain.

Ideal fielding position: Head down, butt down, feet spread wide, hands out, throwing hand above the heel of the glove.

If you were to draw a straight line on the path along which the routine ground ball is traveling, and then you were to draw a line that joined the tips of your shoes, those two lines should be perpendicular at the moment the ball hits your glove. I have heard some instructors teach that the left foot should be slightly forward (assuming you are a right-handed thrower; for lefties, it will be the opposite), but I have to disagree with this. The more your left foot creeps forward, the less able your body will be to react properly to a bad hop. To me, what separates the great defensive infielder from the average defensive infielder is the ability to handle that tricky hop, that four- to six-inch deviation off the anticipated hop. Keeping your left foot back, and, therefore, your weight back, will allow you to react better to the bad hop.

Another problem a young fielder usually has is that he tends to catch the ball either in the middle or on the right side (again, as a right-handed thrower) of his body. As you lower yourself into the fielding position, picture a vertical line running directly in the middle of your two feet. Ideally, you want to catch the ball 6–12 inches to the left of that line, and the reason is this: because your left arm hangs off your left shoulder, it has more room to react quickly on a bad hop. If you field the ball on the right side of the body, your body can get in the way of your left arm, making it difficult to react to the tricky hop. Even catching the ball on the centerline is not good enough; you must field the ball slightly on the left side of your body.

Bending the wrist back to illustrate what the throwing hand should look like in the proper fielding position. If the wrist isn't bent, the fingers become vulnerable to a bad hop.

Finally, with the arms extended, take your throwing hand, spread your fingers as wide as possible, and bend the hand back so it makes a 90-degree angle with your forearm. The hand, in this position, goes directly over the heel of the glove, and it serves two purposes: (1) it will help to protect your upper torso and face from a bad hop and (2) it will often redirect a bad hop into your glove. I, as well as many ballplayers, have had groundballs actually hit my throwing hand and carom into my glove, which is where we want the ball to be anyway, right? But that is possible only when your meat hand is in the proper position. If the hand is on the side of the glove or hanging at your side, it is of no use to you for fielding. Make sure your wrist is bent back so a bad hop doesn't hit the tip of one of your fingers. I saw a player break a finger on a ball like that. If his hand had been bent back, there's no way he would have broken his finger.

Creating Soft Hands

Once the ball hits your glove, you use the "funnel" technique, which means that you pull the glove, the ball, and the throwing hand into your *midsection*. (Another flaw I see in young infielders is that too many of them funnel the ball to the right hip, but the ball *must* be brought to the midsection.) In doing so, you are "giving" with the speed of the ball and developing the "soft hands" that all good infielders have. To make a football comparison, think of a wide receiver making a one-handed catch. Which way does his hand move? Does he stab at the ball, or does he give with the ball? Of course, he gives with it to soften the force at contact. You want the same effect when fielding a groundball.

Funneling the ball into the midsection.

Funneling while keeping the head and body down.

Assuming you have fielded the ball cleanly and it is now in your glove, you technically "redirect" the ball into your right hand, which has been positioned over the glove. When an infielder fields a ball with two hands, the glove doesn't actually close; rather, the ball is more or less deflected into your throwing hand. Once you have the ball securely in your throwing hand, you grab the ball with the four seams, the technique discussed in the pitching section.

Making the Throw

So, once you've taken the "banana route," caught the ball cleanly, and gripped the four seams, you now take a miniature "crow hop" towards first base. If you've ever seen an outfielder catch a fly ball while running towards home plate, he takes a jump, a "crow hop," to maximize the velocity of his throw. In the infield, where you have to be quicker with your throws, you take a "baby crow hop." To do so, you simply take a powerful little hop with your right foot *directly* to first base. Often, you will see an infielder cross his right foot behind his left foot, but when you practice it, do it by taking your right foot *in front of* your left. I can't emphasize enough how important it is to use this quick, powerful "baby crow hop." In doing so, you will see a noticeable difference in the strength and accuracy of your throw.

Finally, there is the follow-through. As you will read in the hitting chapter, the follow-through is important in any action in any sport. The follow-through in baseball, from an infielder's standpoint, is that you "follow" your throw. In other words, after you throw the ball to first base, you literally follow your throwing action by taking a few steps toward first base. This movement will prevent you from simply throwing and recoiling, which often results in inaccurate, weak throws. Once again I cannot illustrate enough how important it is to use your entire body to throw, rather than just your arm strength alone. Certainly, arm strength is very important but that strength must be harnessed. A strong but inaccurate arm is no more useful at times than a weak arm.

Reviewing

In closing, let me summarize the points that I have touched on in this chapter. You must be in the ready position when the ball is approaching the contact zone, and at the point of contact, your body must already be in a state of motion. As the ball is on its way to you, you move ever so slightly towards the baseball in the "banana route." Once you decide to break down and catch the ball, you square your feet to the path of the ball, you lower your head and your butt as much as possible, and you field the ball in front of your body, as opposed to underneath your body. As the ball meets your glove, you "funnel" it into your midsection, and this action creates soft hands. You now take a powerful step towards first base (or the desired base) with your right leg and deliver the baseball. After you release the ball, you follow your throw with your body.

Drills

When I was a sophomore in college, the St. Louis Cardinals drafted our shortstop in the 15th round. Obviously, he must have been a pretty quality infielder, and he was. I used to pick his brain all the time about fielding tips, and he told me about a drill he learned at the Bucky Dent School in Florida. It's really quite simple: take a ball (a tennis ball or a baseball), stand about thirty feet away from solid wall, throw the ball against it, and catch it on the rebound. The drill may sound easy to perform, but can you perform it correctly? By correctly, I mean can you consistently field the ball on the "big hop" or the "short hop" and avoid the "in-between hop?" Eventually, you should be able to field hundreds in a row without missing because, after all, there are no bad hops involved.

Marty Martinez, famed Latin American fielding instructor and scout (he claimed he signed Omar Vizquel to his first contract, though I don't know if that's true), used to talk about the "burnout drill" to which he introduced the nine-time, Gold Glove-winning Vizquel. In this drill he basically took the Bucky Dent drill and sped it up to where the player would throw the ball and catch it as many times as possible at a frantic pace. He said, "C'mon, Bo, I showed this drill to Omar, and he became the best shortstop in baseball. If you can do it for a minute straight without missing, I'll buy you a steak dinner." He was famous for his "steak-dinner" proposition, and many a ballplayer took on the challenge only to find that at about the halfway point, the legs turn into Jell-O. Regardless, it is fun and useful drill, and I wholeheartedly recommend it. (Incidentally, I lasted about 30 seconds before I ran out of gas. No steak for me.)

3

Hitting

Entire books have been written on this single, crucial element of the game. My goal is not to present a new theory of hitting, but to discuss basic matters of technique from a practical standpoint. (This chapter is derived from a short work I produced in 2000 called *The Professional Hitter's Manual*.)

Dispelling the myths of hitting

It is my experience that there is far too much improper teaching going on in the baseball world by people who are unqualified to teach it. Therefore, I want to spend this section dealing with what you may have been told to do somewhere along the way and explaining to you how the traits that make good hitters successful may not be what you think. In other words, first, you have to learn what *not* to do.

Myth #1
You Should Hit with Your Back Elbow Up

You may have heard the term "old wives' tale." Well, this one is an "old father's tale," in that while meaning well, a lot of fathers pass on this bit of misguided advice to their sons. In fact, my father used to tell my younger brother and me to "get the back elbow up" when we were in Little League. Twenty years later, when I asked him why, he said it's because he heard another coach say it to one of his kids. If, when a kid first picks up a bat, he holds his back elbow shoulder-height or higher and has some success with it, then leave him alone. However, very, very few big league hitters hit like that for the simple reason that it is uncom-

Back elbow up. Unless it is natural, this position is usually very uncomfortable.

fortable. It also causes the swing to be longer and slower than necessary.

Myth #2
You Snap Your Wrists at Contact

My coach at the University of North Carolina used the term "buggy-whip" when referring to hitters with quick bats, but this term is misleading. Some hitters, because their swings are so quick, appear to be breaking their wrists at contact, but trust me when I tell you that no professional hitter ever hit the ball with authority this way. Hank Aaron was known for his "quick wrists," a label I have never understood. He had an exceptional weight transfer, which resulted in exceptional bat speed, which gave the appearance of "quick wrists," but that is because during most of his career, there was no slow-action film available to dissect his swing properly. Quick hands? Absolutely. Strong wrists? Absolutely. Quick wrists? Absolutely not. If you don't believe me, go swing a bat against a telephone pole, and look at your hands at the point of contact. If you want to really hit the pole hard, there's only one way to do it, and that is with your hands in a palm-up, palm down position.

Myth #3
Squash the Bug When You Swing

The idea behind this tidbit is to fire your hips, thus rotating on the ball of your back foot, thus "squashing the bug." Part of this is true because hitting is partly rotational, but very, very few hitters ever had any success by simply spinning. Yes, the back foot will spin and squash the bug, but this action must be accompanied by shifting of the weight from the back leg to the front. A weight transfer of some kind is imperative, and if you just spin, there will be *no* weight transfer.

Myth #4
A Hitch in the Swing Is Always Bad

It is bad only if it prevents the hitter from firing on time. Believe it or not, many good hitters have hitches in some way or another, usually for one of two main reasons. First, it may be a timing mechanism that they have had for a long time. The essence of hitting is the ability to arrive at the point of contact on time, and taking away a hitch from a successful hitter is no different than forcing a hitch upon one. Secondly, one law of physics states that an object in motion tends to stay in motion unless acted on by an outside force, and an object at rest tends to stay at rest unless acted on by an outside force. Here's my point: if your hands are slightly moving at the split-second you decide to swing, then you are going to be able to react more quickly. It is the same as a drag race between two cars that start from the exact same point, only one of them is perfectly still and the other is rolling forward ever so slowly until it reaches the starting line. I think we both know which one will fire out quicker.

Myth #5
Big Muscles Equal Big Power

Do you ever notice how some little guys can hit the ball farther than some bigger guys? Sure, some of it is strength, but the bottom line is that bat speed dictates how hard and/or far you hit the ball. Unfortunately, it has been my experience that, like foot speed and arm strength, bat speed can't be improved very much. One of my former teammates, a former Yankee minor leaguer, remembers watching Darryl Strawberry take batting practice and how he could barely see Strawberry's bat coming through the hitting zone because it was so quick. He says watching "Straw" take BP and hit balls through 30-MPH winds in Florida spring training for long homeruns was a sight to behold.

Another former teammate of mine played against Manny Ramirez in a high school tournament, and he said hearing Ramirez's swing was like taking a switch from a tree and hearing the "whoosh" sound it makes as it cuts through the air. That, my friend, is bat speed. Now, not too many hitters have that type of bat speed, so don't worry too much if you don't either. Personally, I stress trying to be as quick with the bat as possible, and although it may not transfer into a ton of homeruns, it will allow you wait on the ball longer, giving you more time to recognize the pitch, and still drive it into the gaps with authority. In other words, you don't necessarily *need* big muscles to hit the ball hard, but you do need to generate a certain amount of bat speed. How you generate it is up to you and your natural ability as a hitter.

Myth #6
Good Hitters Simply See the Ball and Hit It

No one, and I don't care if your last name was Ruth, Mantle, or Gwynn, ever just walked up to the plate, looked for the ball to appear from the pitcher's hand, and hit it hard consistently. There may have been times when a hitter was "in the zone" and it seemed that simple to him, but all good hitters have an approach. They look for certain pitches from a certain pitcher in a certain count, and if they don't get it, they take it. One former teammate of mine played with Larry Walker, 1997 NL MVP and multiple-time batting champion, and he said that Walker would sometimes look for a certain pitch over the course of *three at-bats* until he got it, and when he did, he'd hammer it. Certainly, that type of discipline is an advanced skill—far too advanced for the amateur ballplayer—but it goes to show the type of discipline good hitters develop. Good hitters know what pitches they themselves handle well and which ones they do not, and they generally swing at the ones they can hit hard and don't swing at the ones that they can't. Obviously, this approach sounds more simple than it is, but having your own personal approach is as basic as having your own bat: you wouldn't walk up to the plate without either, would you?

Myth #7
Good Hitters Don't Strike Out

Let me explain. In order to get a pitch in your "happy zone," a Ted Williams term for the specific part of the strike zone that a hitter handles very well, you may have to look at three or four pitches, some of them strikes, before you get the one you're looking for. Therefore, good, patient hitters hit deep into the count, sometimes taking a marginally good pitch or pitches in search of the perfect pitch. Before they know it, they have two strikes on them, and now they're in defense mode instead of attack mode. While they may have failed in that particular at-bat to get the pitch that they wanted, for my money, a patient approach will get you better pitches to hit over the course of a long season.

As an example of the impatient hitter, take Joe Sewell, a light-hitting middle infielder from the 1930s. He had a career AB-to-strikeout ratio of 63-to-1 over his career, he was a lifetime .300 hitter, and he used the same bat for something like eleven years. Great hitter, right? Well, why hadn't you heard of him until right now? For starters, he obviously wasn't swinging very hard or he would have broken his lucky bat by just missing the sweet spot. Also, he never drove in many runs because he had to have swung at too many pitcher's pitches early in the count and not waited for a better one to hit. My point is that one of the risks of looking for a perfect pitch is that you may find yourself behind in the count from time to time, but I still believe you'll be better off over the long haul.

Myth #8
Good Hitters Can Handle Every Pitch in a Pitcher's Repertoire

Everyone remembers John Kruk ("I ain't an athlete, lady, I'm a baseball player") as the long-haired, beer-swilling redneck who went on *David Letterman* quite a bit, but did you know that he ended his career as a .300 lifetime hitter? Guys like Reggie Jackson, Mickey Mantle, and Barry Bonds can't make that claim, yet in his autobiography, Kruk says that he couldn't hit a big-league curveball unless he was guessing it. That should tell you two things: (1) a big-league curveball is very difficult to hit and (2) good hitters make their livings off pitchers' mistakes. Even Hall-of-Famer Kirby Puckett admitted that he would beat up on the fourth and fifth starters and middle relievers on a team's pitching staff because those pitchers tend to be the weak links. **Good pitching will always stop good hitting.** Like Puckett said, when facing the ace of a staff, "Take your 0-for-3 with a walk or a 1-for-4, be happy with it, and come out the next day ready to beat up on a lesser quality pitcher."

Myth #9
Good Hitters Cover All 17 Inches of the Plate

Let me start off this one with a story. Back in the 1920s Rogers Hornsby hit over .400 for five years in a row, from 1920 through 1924. Not too bad, huh? Well, apparently some young, hot-shot pitcher had just been called up from the minors and was facing the venerable Hornsby for the first time. He uncorked his first pitch, a pitch he thought had caught the corner, and when the umpire called it a ball, the pitcher just glared at him. He threw the next pitch in the same place, and, once again, the ump called it a ball, and, once again, the hurler glared at him. Biting his tongue, the rookie threw his third straight pitch in the exact same place as the first two only to hear "ball three" from the umpire, and Hornsby hadn't so much as flinched at any of the offerings. The pitcher stormed down of the mound demanding to know what the umpire was looking at. The umpire removed his mask and uttered calmly, "Young man, when you throw a strike, Mr. Hornsby will let you know." Now, that makes for a nice story, but you can bet the ranch that Hornsby didn't win two Triple Crowns by swinging at pitches right on the corner or just barely off the plate—those are definitely *not* hitter's pitches.

Similarly, I know a college coach who claimed that when he was in college, where he was quite a good hitter judging by his numbers, if he was looking for a fastball and it was a strike, he could hit it hard somewhere. Although I didn't say it at the time, I didn't believe him. Now, let's say I give him the benefit of the doubt, and let's say that with an aluminum bat and an average college fastball of 82 MPH, he could do it, but no way in hell he could do it with a wooden bat and a 90 MPH fastball. Guys named Boggs can't even do that.

Myth #10
You Will Always Receive Good Hitting Instruction

If you've ever played sports, period, you know this is simply not the case. Personally, no one told me anything worthwhile about hitting until I reached my sophomore year of college. I mentioned at the beginning of this manual that good, qualified hitting coaches are few and far between. Many men who consider themselves to be "hitting coaches" have never played beyond high school or the small-college level, and thus, what they teach may work against inferior pitching but not when the men on the mound can really pitch well. Also, many coaches who were good hitters when they played are so far removed from playing that they forget how difficult, both mentally and physically, hitting can be. For example, my coach at the University of North Carolina during my freshman year fell into this category. He actually played some minor league ball, but he fell into the "justification of paycheck theory" category of coaches who believe that because they are being paid to coach, they must invent things to teach in order to appease their bosses and to ease their own minds.

The mechanics of the swing

When it comes to the actual mechanics of the swing, less is more. By that, I mean that unless a hitter is really doing something wrong, drastic changes usually do more harm than good. Minor changes—moving the hands an inch or two, a different model bat, etc.—are good to experiment with, but major overhauls tend to be counterproductive. As I mentioned in the beginning, some people may say that hitting is mostly mental, and that's true once you get to a certain age and ability level. To reach that point, though, you have to burn your swing into your muscle-memory with proper technique and lots of practice. Those two facets, proper technique and practice, have to go hand in hand, and let me tell you why.

Imagine trying to circumnavigate the globe in the days before maps. Now, you may have all the time and desire in the world to see your trip through, and you could blindly set out on the dangerous seas in pursuit of your destination. You may or may not make it, but it will take you a long time either way just to find out. Chances are, though, you'll be blown off course and spend the rest of your life wandering the seven seas in search of your goal. Wouldn't it be easier if you had a map to rely on? The seas will still be stormy and the winds still fierce, but you will have a much better chance of completing your journey. You be the captain, and I'll be the navigator.

I have broken up this section into the components of the swing, and they are as follows: the stance, the stride, the launch position, the unloading, the point of contact, and the follow-through. These steps occur chronologically within the swing, and so we'll deal with them in that order.

The Stance

When I hear a hitting coach spend an inordinate amount of time teaching the stance, I can pretty much write him off as a hitting coach. If stance were that critical, all big league hitters would be identical in their stances. In fact, I have followed baseball so closely over the years that if there were a way to remove skin color and jerseys from the star players—those who appear the most frequently on the highlight shows—and try to identify them based solely on their stance and swings, I believe I could choose correctly 80–90 percent of the time. Part of that is due to my being a student of the game but more so to the individuality of the good big league hitters.

In the stance comfort is the most important thing, and balance is a close second. Every once in a while, you'll see a Rickey Henderson or Brian Jordan (c. 1999), both of whom rest a lot of weight on their back legs. Or you'll see a Jeff Bagwell hitting out of a pronounced crouch, but

A balanced, comfortable stance.

the key is to avoid the extremes, *i.e.*, too straight up and down, too crouched, weight too far forward, weight too far back. As for where to stand in the batter's box, again, try to avoid the extremes, and work it out for yourself. Most kids will naturally assume the most comfortable position and place for their body types, thus eliminating the need to make a drastic change.

Another facet of hitting that gets far too much attention is the grip. I have heard a coach debate the grip for 15 or 20 minutes, again prompting me to write him off as a qualified hitting coach. These types of

Top left: The proper grip. *Middle*: Still too much space between the hands in the grip. *Right*: Far too much space between the hands in the grip. With the hands like this, it is very difficult to maximize bat speed. *Bottom left*: Gripping the bat in the fingers (recommended). *Right*: Gripping the bat in the palm of the hand (not as effective).

coaches usually speak tirelessly of stances and grips to cover up the fact that they really don't know what they are talking about. The only thing I will say about the grip is that ideally, you should grip the bat with the fingers, not in the palm. When I say the fingers, I mean right where the fingers meet the hand. Any lower and I think you lose range of motion, which can cause you to lose bat speed. Once again, comfort is the most important thing.

The Stride

Moving along, let's look at the stride. Even though some hitters, like Jim Edmonds, don't stride a lot of the time, we'll still call it that. A common question I get from young hitters is, "When do you stride?" That's like asking, "When do you pick up the ball from the pitcher?" All I can say is that it is something that each hitter must figure out for

Hands *not* in the ideal palm-up, palm-down position. Rolling the wrists too soon can severely hamper bat speed.

himself, and timing is everything. If you stride too soon or too late, you probably won't do anything productive on that particular swing, and successful pitchers make their livings by upsetting that timing. One of the only things you, as a hitter, can control is when to take that stride, and no matter what type of pitch the pitcher decides to throw, your stride will take place at the same time for that particular pitcher (whether the pitch arrives at the time you are expecting it to arrive is a different story, which is what makes hitting so frustratingly difficult).

Like the stance, you want to avoid extremes in the stride, in other words, too close too the plate, too far "in the bucket," too long, or too short. Again, there are exceptions to the rule, like Jeff Bagwell, who sometimes actually strides *backwards* an inch or two. (You have to wonder how Bagwell, 1994 NL MVP, has been so successful with such unconventional mechanics. I actually heard him joke that a whole generation of Houston boys are going to be striding backwards during their baseball careers.) As for the other extreme, I played with and against 1989 NL MVP Kevin Mitchell, who, while being no taller than 5'11", took about a 15" stride, which appears to be grossly out of proportion with his height, but watching him hit — heck, *hearing* him hit — made me a believer. The bottom line is that you have to find what maximizes your own ability, just as Bagwell and Mitchell have done.

The Launch Position

Next comes the launch position, which refers to the point in your swing when your stride-foot hits the ground. It is at this point that your mind tells you whether you are going to swing or not, so it is imperative that you are ready to fire, for any wasted motion can really mess up your timing. Now, I am no stickler when it comes to styles of hitting (leg kicks, short strides, one-handed follow-throughs, etc.), but if there were one style I would stress, it is having the *hands high* at the launch position. By high, I mean as high as the individual feels is comfortable without causing any tension in the neck and shoulders. Basically, I have only one reason why I believe this to be so important: it will force you to attack down through the hitting zone, making your swing shorter and quicker. Trust me when I say it is almost impossible to catch up to a 90-mph fastball by swinging up at it. The shorter your swing is, the quicker it will be, which will give you an edge when it comes to pitch selection. Simply put, the longer you can wait, the longer you can watch the ball before you decide to swing, and the less chance you will be fooled by the pitch.

When the front foot hits the ground, you should try to keep it

The launch position: hands back and high, weight evenly distributed, eyes level, head of the bat directly over the head.

closed (parallel to the top of home plate) as much as possible. It will probably open a little bit, but any more than a two-inch deviation from the ball of the foot to the heel in relation to a parallel line causes leaking. Leaking refers to any forward movement or opening that occurs prior to the snapping open of the swing. One way to keep from leaking is to imagine keeping your stride-foot knee closed. You can accomplish this action by turning the instep of the stride foot downward slightly. In fact, my parents have a picture of me from my sophomore year of college in their living room of me in that exact same position — the front foot is slightly open, but the knee is definitely closed. Incidentally, that must have been one of the many things I did right that spring when I hit .423.

The Unloading

So, you've settled into your most comfortable, balanced stance, you've taken your stride, and your front foot is down and closed. Now, it's time to unload. Once you determine where the pitch is going and how fast it's going — all done in .4 seconds, mind you — you are ready to swing. One of the most basic tenets of hitting that all hitting coaches (the good ones, at least) agree on is that the hips lead the hands through the zone. By that I mean that the force generated by the combined weight shift of the body and the rotation of the hips is transferred into the hands, wrists, and arms and then directed into the desired part of the strike zone. Put simply, the legs and hips produce the power, and the hands direct it. Sometimes, when I would take a pitch, I would feel my lower half starting to rotate before my upper half, and that's when I knew everything was working properly. On the other hand, I can still remember seeing a guy trying to make Virginia Tech's team as a walk-on during fall practice, and he was swinging in the on-deck circle with his hips coming through the zone *after* his hands. Needless to say that with those mechanics, he didn't make the team.

Another important term that good hitting coaches use deals with "staying inside the ball." This term is perhaps the most difficult to explain without my being there to demonstrate it in person, but think about the back elbow dragging over the back hip as tightly as possible during the swing. Similar to a figure skater spinning on the ice, the closer the limbs can stay to the axis, the faster the entire body will rotate. Obviously, you aren't going to spin anywhere near as fast as a figure skater, but the same law of physics (The Law of Conservation of Angular Momentum) applies. The farther away from the body the arms travel, the less quickly you can swing the bat.

Left: Attacking *inside* the ball. Notice the back elbow remaining close to the body as the hands take the bat to the ball. *Right*: Hitting around the ball. When the back elbow moves away from the body, the hitter loses a significant amount of bat speed.

Another critical part of the actual swing is head discipline. Everybody knows to "watch the ball," but some hitting coaches will overemphasize it by saying that your head should actually go down an inch or two, and I'll buy that. Certainly, you don't it want to go down so far that you lose your balance, but the idea is that you can't hit what you don't see. Personally, I know for a fact that I had better head discipline from the left side, which may explain in part why I was a better hitter from that side for my entire career.

Finally, let me add that if you think about swinging *down* at the ball — remember my insistence on keeping the hands as high as is comfortable? — it will help you stay inside the ball. In reality, the swing will end up being level, but *thinking* down will help eliminate any loops in the swing.

The Point of Contact

Once the unloading occurs and the bat has traveled on its path through the hitting zone, you are ready for the moment of truth — the point of contact. I mentioned "staying inside the ball" and how difficult the concept is to explain without my being there. The same is true for the point of contact. Because the entire swing happens so quickly, the only way to see what the ideal point of contact should look like is with video footage or still photos. I have seen my fair share of slow-motion

Attacking the ball with the barrel above the hands as long as possible.

swings in my lifetime, and I believe I can explain what the point of contact should look like.

Because there is so much confusion — and, as a result, so many falsehoods surrounding the point of contact — perhaps I could have included these next two paragraphs in the "dispelling the myths" section, but I chose to include the themes here. One ill-explained part about the point of contact is where, in fact, contact should occur. I hear a lot of coaches talk about making contact "in front of home plate" or "over home plate," but neither of these references makes any sense to me. According to John Kruk, Tony Gwynn of the San Diego Padres stood so far forward in the batter's box that his stride foot would actually land outside of the box. Therefore, common sense says that every time he made contact, it would occur in front of home plate. Luis Gonzales of the Arizona Diamondbacks, on the other hand, stands on the back line of the batter's box, and unless a pitch fooled him badly, he would always make contact *behind* home plate. To me, your front foot is the best reference point for ideal contact. Assuming your balance is correct, you want to make contact with a fastball over the middle of the plate *directly over* your front foot. If the pitch is slightly outside, then contact will happen a few inches *behind* your front foot, and if the pitch is slightly inside, contact will take place slightly *in front of* your front foot.

The other vague, ambiguous term that hitting coaches use is "extension." It is true that extension is imperative (Charley Lau listed "Getting Proper Extension" as one of his Ten Absolutes of Good Hitting), but no one seems to know how to get extension or when it should happen. Obviously, as a hitter, you don't want to be "chicken-winged" (a term for being badly jammed by a pitch in which the lead arm is noticeably bent at contact) but you also don't want both of your arms to be extended at the point of contact, either. At contact, ideally, you want your lead arm to be *ever so slightly* flexed and the back arm to be bent at roughly a 90-degree angle. I call this the "power position." In this posi-

When both arms are extended like this, the ball should have already left the bat. A hitter who tries to reach this position at exactly the point of contact leaves himself little room for error.

tion, you are (1) in your physically strongest position to deliver a blow to the baseball and (2) able to make contact and hit through the ball. Think about it: if you made contact with both arms fully extended, you have nothing left to hit through the ball. Therefore, extension — when both arms become fully extended — occurs well after contact and well after the ball has left the bat.

The Follow-Through

The last part of the swing deals with the follow-through, and before I touch on the importance of it in baseball, let me state a universal athletic truth: a follow-through ensures proper mechanics *before* the specific action, not after. A basketball player may hold his shooting hand in the "gooseneck" position after making a game-winning shot to pose for the crowd (think of the last shot of Michael Jordan's career with the Chicago

The power position: back leg bent, front leg locked, lead arm locked, back arm bent, head down and over back thigh, palm-up/palm-down.

Bulls), but he did it originally to ensure that all his mechanics were sound up to and including the release of the ball. The same idea applies in baseball. The follow-through makes certain that you don't prematurely choke off the swing, which results in the top hand rolling over too soon, significantly impairing your ability to hit the ball with authority.

Now, there are two schools of thought on the baseball follow-through — top hand on and top hand off — and there seems to be a lot of confusion regarding the latter. Therefore, let me put it point-blank: you remove the top hand *only* when it begins to restrict your follow-through (usually, the top hand releases near the front ear). To explain further, look at two of the more feared hitters of the 1990s, Frank Thomas and Mike Piazza. These guys hit for both power and average yet have two totally different styles and follow-throughs. Frank Thomas is 6'5", 250 lbs. and strong as an ox, but he is so muscle-bound through the chest and shoulders that he *has* to take the top hand off the bat in

This is an example of taking the top hand off too soon. Doing so can severely hinder a hitter's power.

A high, one-handed finish. removing the top hand allows the hitter's head to stay down longer and ensure a complete swing.

A two-handed follow-through. Notice how strained a hitter can look with both hands on the bat.

his follow-through or else he couldn't properly finish his swing. Piazza, on the other hand, while strong in his own right, is evidently much more flexible, which allows him to keep both hands on the bat for his entire follow-through. The point is that you must —*must*— hit through the ball, and like so many other parts of the swing, it's up to you to determine what works best for you.

My three rules of good hitting

In this section I will tell you the keys that helped me maximize my ability as a hitter, and perhaps one, or all, of them may help you to become a better hitter. I cannot speak for other players I played with or against in my career, and it would be foolish of me to assume I know what made them successful hitters. All I know is what worked for Bo Durkac. To me, the following three rules allowed me to reach my maximum potential:

1. Don't swing at balls and pitcher's pitches
2. Murder the mistakes
3. Battle with two strikes

Don't Swing at Balls and Pitcher's Pitches

To me, developing a good eye at the plate is something that always made sense to me and therefore became a top priority. I know for a fact that in only two seasons since my freshman year of college did I have more strikeouts than walks in a season. Now, I've never been the swiftest of runners, so you may be wondering what good it does to walk to first base if you can't steal second, which I couldn't. Well, the more times you are on base, the better chance you have to score. Everyone knows about the stat that exists for on-base percentage, but there isn't one for the percentage of times you score after reaching base. I'll bet you dollars to donuts, though, that percentage-wise, it is easier to go from first to home than it is to get from home to first. Ted Williams was never more than an average runner, but he led the AL in runs scored seven times in one eight-year stretch, mostly due to his unbelievable OBP, which is #1 all-time at .483. Therefore, let's look at the benefits of working the count.

First of all, I never saw the point in swinging at balls. Making solid contact is tough enough when you're swinging at pitches in the strike zone, let alone ones that aren't. One thing I was always good at is not swinging at breaking balls out of the strike zone. I have a theory about breaking balls and it goes like this: if you could monitor the total number of breaking pitches thrown over the course of a major league season, it is my guess that only 33 percent or so of them would be called a strike if the hitters didn't swing at them. My point is that most of the time, a breaking ball is designed to *look* like a strike, but by the time the catcher catches it, it is a ball. Hence, if you can train yourself to take those pitches, you'll eventually find yourself in more hitters' counts, which will ultimately make you a better hitter. When you find yourself in a lot of 2–0 and 3–1 counts, you know that your approach is working well for you because those counts usually mean a fastball is coming, and every good hitter who ever played lived for those counts.

Also, there is a team aspect of looking at a lot of pitches. What separates middle relievers from starters on a pitching staff? Easy, right? Starters, the vast majority of the time, are better simply pitchers than the middle relievers. Knowing this, wouldn't it make sense to try to get the starting pitcher out of the game as soon as possible and face a lesser quality pitcher? Of course it would. The more pitches a pitcher has to throw, the more quickly he will fatigue. When a pitcher fatigues, he either starts making mistakes up in the strike zone or is removed for a middle reliever. In both cases, your team gains an advantage.

Finally, let me summarize by saying that most good hitters have "two types of discipline." First is the more basic one, the knowledge of the strike zone. Knowing what is a ball and what is a strike is obviously an important fundamental of hitting. Second, good hitters develop a type of discipline in knowing what they handle well and what they don't. Remember that just because the pitch will be called a strike doesn't mean you have to swing at it.

Murder the Mistakes

OK. You've spit on the balls and pitcher's pitches, and you now find yourself in a count where you can expect a fastball with great certainty, and as it turns out, here it comes. Even though a pitcher almost never wants to throw the ball right over the middle of the plate, sometimes the pitch will end up there, and these pitches are called mistakes. Now, this is where your hours of practice pay off. You've finely tuned your swing for this one moment when you have the pitcher right where you want him, the pitch is on its way, and you hit a screaming line drive into the gap for a double. Let me tell you that there are not too many better feelings than developing your own plan of attack at the plate and getting the results you envisioned on a consistent basis. For some guys the result may be a towering homerun, for others a sharp single up the middle, but all I can do as a hitting instructor is put you in a position to hit the ball as hard and far as your ability allows you and to do it as consistently as possible. You'd be surprised at the number of big league hitters who can only handle certain pitches or certain parts of the strike zone, yet they stay in the majors for years because when they get that pitch, they hammer it. It doesn't do you any good to work the count, get the pitch you're looking for, and then foul it off or pop it up. Again, that's where the practice comes in. You have to be able to react in that split-second to get the sweet spot of the bat on the sweet spot of the ball with as much force behind it as you can.

Battle with Two Strikes

Look, hitting is hard. Period. You are going to go through stretches when it seems as though every pitch is on the black, when every time that you are sure he going to throw a fastball, here comes the curve. Or maybe you are getting the pitch you are looking for, but for some reason, maybe a mechanical one, you're fouling it off instead of killing it. Just what you needed — more mental anguish. It is at this point that you find yourself in a lot of two-strike counts and at the pitcher's mercy. Hitting with two strikes is tough, but not as tough as some make it out to be. In today's game a lot of hitters still take a full swing with two strikes whereas 25 years ago, striking out was an ego-bruiser. Personally, I didn't like striking out, so I did what I could to avoid it.

The first thing I would do was psyche myself up mentally, telling myself that I am *not* going to strike out (it doesn't always work, as I struck out more than once in my career). The more tough pitches you can foul off, the more likely the pitcher is going to be to make a mistake. That ability to get just barely a piece of a nasty two-strike pitch may be what ultimately separates the below average hitters from the good ones. The good ones spoil tough pitch after tough pitch until they either draw a walk or get a mistake that they can hit hard; the poor ones swing and miss and strike out. The second thing is to choke up on the bat, maybe an inch. It will make you just a bit quicker. Then, I spread out my stance a little more, so I could take a shorter stride, meaning less wasted movement. Finally, and most importantly, I looked for the ball on the outer-third of the plate. There two main reasons for this. One is that if you are looking for the ball away from you, you can hit the fastball away from you and any offspeed pitch because you will wait longer and thus see it longer.

A "flat" bat can give a hitter a quicker, more direct route to the ball, but it can also result in a lot of ground balls to the "pull" side of the field.

A "vertical" bat causes a long, loopy swing which results in weak fly balls.

You will, however, have trouble with the fastball on the inside-third, but like I said earlier, no hitter can cover the entire plate. If, on the other hand, your sights are on the inner third of the plate, the only pitch you can handle is the fastball on the inner third of the plate. Anything offspeed or any fastball away from you will be very difficult to hit because you will have already committed to the inner part of the plate.

Secondly, and this is one of the reasons why I feel I am qualified to teach hitting and others aren't. I was in the trenches, and I realized that most pitchers can't throw to the inside corner with the same accuracy that they can to the outside corner. Mostly, it's due to the fact then when trying to pitch inside, a pitcher has very little margin for error, because a mistake results in either a hit batsman or a pitch right over the heart of the plate. Therefore, doesn't it make sense to look for the part of the plate to where most pitchers feel more comfortable throwing?

Fundamentals vs. styles

I mentioned before how there is far too much improper hitting instruction going on in the baseball world, and a lot of it revolves around the teaching of styles of hitting as opposed to fundamentals of hitting. Remember, a fundamental is something that *has* to be done by a good hitter; a style is how he himself implements that fundamental. Below, I have compiled a chart to explain the differences.

Fundamental	Style	Example
Comfortable stance	Crouch	Jeff Bagwell
	Backward lean	Rickey Henderson
Weight transfer	Leg kick	Juan Gonzalez, Ruben Sierra
	Short stride	Jim Edmonds
	Big stride	Kevin Mitchell
Bat speed	Choking up	Barry Bonds
	Hand on knob	Kevin Mitchell
Follow-through/ extension	One-handed	Frank Thomas
	Two-handed	Mike Piazza
	High finish	Will Clark, Jim Edmonds
	Low finish	Mike Schmidt, Glenallen Hill

The reason I included this chart is to show you some of the important fundamentals of hitting and how some good big league hitters have executed those fundamentals into their own swings. It is important to remember that you must learn good fundamentals of hitting and incorporate them into your own personal swing with your own personal style. In the future, if you have a coach who forces you to hit out of a crouch or to take the top hand off the bat in your follow through, you know you can pretty much let his words go in one ear and out the other.

Drills

Many times, young players will ask me about what drills are effective in making a hitter better, and again, I think my experience as a professional has allowed me to distinguish the worthwhile drills from the "gimmicks," as I call them. I've seen a lot of useless drills and a lot of good ones, so I pass on my two favorites to you. Let me add that tees and front-toss are designed to "groove" your swing, *i.e.*, to develop muscle memory. I personally never worked on hitting off-speed pitches in drills because the only way to become proficient in handling off-speed stuff is to *play*. Game situations are where you develop your plate discipline, your pitch recognition, and above all, your instincts. Don't get too caught up in fiddling around with junk pitches in practice.

The Hansen Drill

This one is named after Terrel Hansen, a former teammate of mine, who introduced me to the drill. It's difficult to explain without my being there, so bear with me.

The idea of this exercise is to make your hands get "inside the ball." Remember how important I said that is earlier. Here's how the drill goes. You get in the typical long batting cage with a home plate and tee. Set up the plate like normal, like there is a pitcher's mound at the far end of the cage. Now, set your tee on home plate. (If you don't have a home plate, just envision where it would be — or make one out of tape — and set the tee there). Now, if you're a right-handed hitter, line up your feet with an imaginary line through the tips of your shoes and through the base of the tee and parallel to the first base line. You got it so far? Next, position your feet so when you take your stride, your stride foot lands about 6–8 inches from the base of the tee. Assuming you've done this from the beginning, you should be in the launch position, with your shoulders and feet forming lines parallel to the first base line. (If you're lefty, just do the same things, but with the third base line). Now, the idea is to take a swing that brings your hands *above* and *inside* the ball and *across* the front of your body. You must force your hands to travel right in front of your navel. The ideal swing will result in driving the ball to the back of the cage without hitting the top, the floor, or either side first.

The drill will feel extremely awkward at first, but that's because you've probably never done something like this before. As an old saying goes, "The ball doesn't lie." If you can consistently hit line drives off the back of the cage — without cheating with your feet, of course — then you will have developed a nice, inside-the-ball swing. I can't emphasize enough how important staying inside the ball is. As Mike Schmidt says, "It will create room in your swing." It will result in a shorter, quicker swing, which will result in making you less susceptible to inside fastballs, which will allow you take away more of the outside part of the plate, which in turn, will make you a better hitter.

The Hansen drill: notice the imaginary straight line between the tips of the toes and the base of the tee.

The Front-Toss Drill

The other drill I love is the "front-toss" drill. Take an L-screen and a chair to sit on, and put the L-screen about 20 feet from home plate. First, turn the screen so that tall part of it is to the middle of the cage to provide maximum protection. Now, line up the screen so that an imaginary line through the tosser's arm, when sticking out from behind the screen, will split the plate right

The Hansen drill: notice the bat squared up to the ball, allowing the hitter to drive the ball to the back of the cage.

down the middle. Don't worry; the tosser will have plenty of time to return his arm behind the L-screen after releasing the ball. Tip: Turn the L-screen slightly so any sharply hit ball won't ricochet off the screen and hit the batter in his follow-through.

Have your partner sit on the chair and with a *consistent*, underhanded motion, have him toss the ball firmly into the hitting zone. The drill is rather simple, but I've seen a lot of guys do it improperly, and then they develop bad habits. The arm motion must be the same every time, something that the batter can time. As I said earlier, the only thing a hitter can time at the plate is the release of the ball; how fast it gets there is another story. But in drills, when you are trying to groove your swing, timing is of the essence and must be virtually eliminated as a variable. Also, the velocity of the tossed ball must simulate game speed. It won't do you any good to lob the ball with an arc on it. How many fastballs have you ever seen with a hump to them? If the toss is too slow, you'll find yourself stepping closer to the plate on the outside pitch and away from the plate if it's inside, and contrary to what some coach may have told you, that's impossible to do in a game situation. When the person tossing the ball gets good at it, you can have him toss inside and outside to simulate game-type fastballs. Remember, don't get too caught up in having the tosser trying to get you out; the idea is to duplicate the same swing over and over again so when you get that nice, meaty fastball in a game, you take that same swing you've honed in the batting cage and crush the ball.

In closing, let me add a few points and bits of advice. (1) I was never a fan of "live" pitching for practice. Basically, it can be too erratic and not give you enough quality swings. Once in a while, live BP is okay, but when you are trying to groove your swing, you need a steady diet of hittable, easily timed strikes. Most BP pitchers can't do that. (2) It's far better to take 100 quality swings at 100 quality tosses in a workout than 100 quality swings and 100 "tired" swings because "tired" swings lead to bad habits. Whenever I work with a hitter, I constantly remind him of that. I tell him, "It's not a race. It's not about how many swings you can take in a half-hour. It's about quality, not quantity." (3) Just as a basketball player who takes 200 jumps shots a day must still play pickup games to incorporate his shooting into a game situation, you must play as many games per year as you can. All the drills in the world will indeed groove your swing, but the only way to learn how to hit a curveball in a game is by seeing curveballs in a game over and over again. I know I played at least 90 games a year for ten years, and there is no substitute for game experience. I recently came up with a quotation to summarize this thought: "You learn to hit the fastball in practice and the curveball in games." Remember that. I promise if you practice these two drills religiously and *correctly*, you'll soon get the results you are seeking.

4

Catching

by Josh McAffee

In the Arizona Diamondbacks' first-ever amateur draft in 1996, they selected catcher Josh McAffee in the fourth round. He spent four years in the Diamondbacks organization and parts of two others with Texas, Houston, and the New York Mets, reaching AA in 2000. I had the good fortune of playing with and befriending him in 2001 when he joined the Sonoma County Crushers. A superb defensive catcher with a powerful arm, "Mac" was the logical choice to author this section on catching.

The art of catching

Catching can be considered an art form. There is no other player on the field with more responsibility than the catcher. Not only is a catcher involved in every pitch, but he is also the only player with a view of the whole field. He can see every facet of the game, which is why he is the leader on the field. It is up to catchers to keep the infielders on their toes, letting them know the situation or even directing them to their respective positions on the field. When it comes to pitchers, catchers are also responsible for their well-being. It is their job to keep them in line, giving them a kick in the ass if they need it, or just a pat on the back to calm them down. It is also up to catchers to deal with the umpire behind the plate. A catcher has to let him know of all his missed calls while still staying on his good side.

Catching also comes with some bumps and bruises, and mental toughness is ever bit as important as physical skills. Anyone can catch a game feeling 100 percent, but it is a select few that can come back the next day feeling only 60 percent and still give it everything they have.

The ability to catch day after day is what separates an average catcher from a great catcher. Remember, strapping on the gear everyday is not a position for the meek.

Brian Butterfield, former third base coach for both the Arizona Diamondbacks and New York Yankees and currently a coach with the Toronto BlueJays, once said to me, "Baseball is the slowest game on earth, but once the ball is put in play, baseball is the fastest game on earth." This is one of the most accurate statements of the game I have ever heard and especially true when it comes to catching. There are so many aspects of the game going on when trying to catch a 90 MPH fastball, to block a nasty curve ball in the dirt, or to throw out a jackrabbit trying to steal second base, and the mechanics of catching come into play on each pitch. The mechanics will help with the success and consistency at this demanding position. In this chapter I will talk about the three most important aspects of catching: receiving, blocking and throwing. I will also discuss other areas of catching which will be helpful to the development of a catcher.

The Stances

There are two different types of catcher stances. The first stance is the "relaxed" catcher stance. I will use the relaxed stance when there are

Receiving the ball in the "relaxed position."

no runners on base. The idea behind this stance is to be as comfortable as possible (in order to conserve energy for the other stance) but still in a strong athletic position with throwing hand either behind my back or behind my right foot. The reason I put my throwing hand behind my back or behind my right foot is to keep foul tips from coming in contact with my throwing hand

The second stance is the "ready" stance. I use this stance with runners on base or with two strikes on any given hitter. The difference between the relaxed stance and the ready stance is that instead of putting the throwing hand behind the back, I will put it behind my glove. My throwing hand has to be readily available for blocking and throwing purposes, which I will get into later in this chapter. Also, my throwing hand, when behind the glove, is in a closed-fist position while keeping it relaxed as possible. This position will help protect it in the chance of a foul tip. The final adjustment from the relaxed stance to the ready stance involves raising up my butt approximately three to four inches higher in the ready stance in order to keep myself in a good athletic position. All of these minor changes will greatly improve my ability to block and throw from the ready position.

Preparing to receive the ball in the ready position. Notice that the throwing hand is completely behind the glove, which helps to avoid a foul ball off the throwing hand.

Receiving the ball in the "ready position."

Proper placement of the throwing hand in the relaxed position.

Giving Signs

When giving signs to the pitcher, keeping everyone on the field from knowing what pitch is being thrown is paramount. I start by keeping my legs close together, which will hide the signs from the opposing first and third base coaches. To get to this position, my feet must start no more than six inches apart. Next, I place my glove on the outside of the left knee, which will help obstruct the view of the third base coach. From here, I am now ready to give signs to the pitcher. It is imperative that my right hand is tucked as close to the cup area as possible. (There is nothing wrong with having one of your coaches check you from the first and third base coaching boxes.) Also, pay attention to the opposing first and third base coaches. I can usually tell if the opposition's coaches are trying to pick up my signs just by watching them. If their eyes are fixated on me while I am giving signs, there is a pretty good chance that they are attempting to steal them.

Receiving

To me, receiving is the most important aspect of catching. Glenn Sherlock, the catching rover for the Arizona Diamondbacks when I was with them, once told me, "A good catcher is one that no one notices". This statement is especially true when it comes to receiving. If a catcher is dropping three to four balls every inning or running to the backstop to pick up missed balls every other pitch, the fans notice. However, if every ball is caught and blocked there is no acknowledgment of a good job catching. Instead the catcher becomes an anonymous "man behind the mask," which appears to be a thankless job to the layman. Only those who have strapped on the gear themselves are able to acknowledge a job well done.

Target

The first consideration when receiving is a good target. I always give a big target that is positioned in the center of my body roughly knee high to the hitter. Now, it's not enough just to throw the mitt up there and hope the pitcher hits it. I need to show the pitcher the full pocket of the glove. Pitchers, the delicate creatures they are, love it when they have a big target to throw to; it gives them a feeling of security.

When giving a proper target, it is critical to start out with the catching elbow down, as opposed to sticking out to the side. To set the catching hand in the proper position, I will point my fingers toward the pitcher, and I will cock my wrist ever so slightly to the left. Notice,

Proper elbow position when receiving in relaxed position: elbow is down.

Improper elbow position: elbow is up.

though, that this position is not a very good target for the pitcher, so now while keeping the same wrist position, I must then point my glove fingers *up* in order to show the pocket of the glove.

Along with giving a target, I need to stress the importance of keeping the catching elbow pointing *down* as opposed to out to the side. When the elbow is down at the side, the receiving arm is in a stronger position. When my elbow is sticking out to the side, I lose strength in my receiving position because I do not have my body behind my elbow to reinforce my catching arm. As you will see, this technique is especially true when I go to catch pitches on the right side of my body or an outside pitch (to a right-handed hitter). The more elevated the elbow, the weaker the receiving position.

Soft Hands

Soft hands are a necessity in seemingly every sport, but how do they pertain to catching? Also, how does a catcher develop soft hands? At the risk of stating the obvious, soft hands are important because without them a catcher will drop and clank balls off his glove that should normally be caught. To develop soft hands, there are several different techniques to consider. First, start out with the placement of the hand in the catcher's glove. Jamming the hand into the glove almost assures hard hands. The glove must do the catching, not the palm of the hand. Personally, I like to have the lower part of my palm stick out roughly 1–1½ inches out of the glove.

Soft hands can also be attained even before the ball is pitched, and loosening the wrist of the catching hand can help. Most catchers use one of two techniques: the "glove-turn" or the "glove-drop." I personally prefer the glove-turn because it helps with the pitches to the left of my body or the inside corner of the plate (to the right-handed hitter). What I mean (assuming all catchers are right handed) is that if there is a left-handed pitcher with a good curve ball or slider or even a right handed pitcher with a good sinking fast ball, a slight glove-turn just before the ball is pitched (roughly 45° turn or rotation to the left) will relax the hand while putting me in a good position to catch the baseball on the left side of my body. I should note this is a *slight* glove-turn, which will not affect me when catching a baseball to the right of my body or on the outside corner of the plate (to the right-handed hitter).

The "glove-drop" technique is also used by many professional catchers and is very effective when trying to relax or soften the hands. Once the catcher has shown a good target and the pitcher has just

The glove turn: a slight rotation of the glove can help a catcher relax his wrist before receiving the ball.

The glove drop: a drop of the glove can help a catcher relax his wrist before receiving the ball.

released the baseball, he simply relaxes the wrist so the glove drops, and the fingers, which were once pointing up in the air, are now pointing towards the pitcher. The technique of the glove-drop is different for every catcher, but remember that too much of a glove-drop will make it hard to react to the high pitch. I should also note that if a catcher starts his glove-drop too soon, it could take away the target from the pitcher. Both of these techniques are effective; however, each catcher is different, and a conscientious catcher will experiment with both of them in order to find out which works better for him.

The Catch

At the very point that the ball arrives to the glove, it is crucial that I do not reach for the ball. Reaching is taking the glove towards and stabbing at the ball. A good catcher must let the ball come to him for two reasons. The first reason is for our own protection. When I am in my stance, I should be roughly an arm's length away from the hitter. A good way to check the distance is by just reaching out my glove to see if I can touch or come close to the right-handed hitter's knee. At this short distance from the hitter, if I try to reach out and catch the ball, I may be hit by the batter's swing. The second reason not to reach out is for throwing purposes, which I will discuss later.

Sticking Pitches

At more than one point in your career, you may have heard the term, "C'mon! Stick that pitch!" "Sticking a pitch" refers to the ability to catch the ball and hold it at the point at which it is caught. The ball should not carry the glove in *any* direction due to the impact of the baseball. Like a lot of baseball terms, this one is said all the time, yet no one seems able to explain how to do it properly. And, like a lot of techniques in baseball, sticking pitches is easier said than done, but I have picked up a few tricks of the trade to help me.

During my professional career, I had the opportunity to work with Don Wakamatsu, who, during my time with the Arizona Diamondbacks, was a manager and catching coach within the organization. He showed me a few techniques to help stick every pitch within three inches on either side of the plate. Catching pitches down the middle of the plate are fairly easy to stick; however, catching a pitch to the left or right of the body requires some adjustments.

When catching a pitch on the right side of my body or on the outside corner (to a right-handed hitter), I must *lean* slightly to the right

Swaying to the right to catch a pitch on the corner.

Swaying to the left to catch a pitch on the corner.

while taking the glove to the ball. When taking my glove to the ball, I do not reach forward. Rather, I reach to the side. As my hand crosses in front of my body to catch the ball, my fingers must stay pointed towards the pitcher and my elbow down at my side in order to keep the glove in a good position to stick the ball. With pitches on the left side of my body or on the inside part of the plate (to the right-handed hitter), I must *lean* to the left and turn my glove over. Any pitch that is over the left knee or to the left of my body can be caught without rotating the catcher's glove. With balls to the left of the left knee, the 45° rotation of the glove (the glove-turn) before the pitch is thrown will help. I can then just continue the rotation of the glove depending on how low and how inside the pitch is. The key is to keep my wrist as straight and rigid as possible. If my hand cocks back, I will find myself in a weak position, increasing the chance of the ball carrying the glove out of the position in which the ball was initially caught. If I do not turn my glove over on the inside pitch, the only way to catch the pitch is to stick the catching elbow out to the side. If you've ever heard the term "getting handcuffed," you know what I mean. When handcuffed, the catcher catches the ball with the wrong part of the glove, usually on the thumb. It almost sounds like a thud, and he may even "get thumbed" (the painful act of catching the ball directly on the thumb). By turning the glove over, however, he has both eliminated the possibility of "getting thumbed" and improved his chances of sticking the baseball.

Working the Umpire

While I am talking about sticking pitches, I must also throw in the appropriate time and place to do so. In the previous section, I discussed sticking pitches only when the ball is over the plate. Now I will move on to certain situations where a catcher will stick pitches off the plate.

Some instructors may tell catchers to frame or to bring back in all pitches three to four inches off the plate back into the strike zone. A catcher may get away with this when he is dealing with an amateur umpire; however, as I moved up through the levels of baseball, the umpires obviously had a better knowledge of the game — and a better knowledge of the strike zone. They know when a catcher is trying to pull a fast one on them. Because of this, I am not a believer in framing pitches to the point where I am pulling pitches back into the zone. Instead I like to use a trick I have learned to dealing with umpires which works about 70 percent of the time. I start out by catching the ball where it is pitched. If the pitch is anywhere over the plate or on the corners, I will hold it for a "thousand-one" count to show the umpire it is a strike.

Conversely, I will *not* stick pitches off the plate. Instead, I simply throw the ball back to the pitcher quickly. In doing so, I am showing the umpire that I know the pitch is a ball. After repeating this for four to five innings, the umpire becomes accustomed to the fact I am holding all strikes and quickly throwing back all non-strikes. In other words, I develop a certain trust, if you will, with the umpire. Then, later in the game, I can expand the strike zone for our pitcher by holding pitches three to four and sometimes even five to six inches off the plate by holding these pitches for a "thousand-one" count. Although I am eradicating the trust of the umpire (although I wouldn't consider it to be a severe breach because I am trying to alter his strike zone without his knowing), this subtle expansion of the strike may get my pitcher a borderline strike or two towards the end of the game. This technique does not work every time because every umpire is different. Sometimes, though, I can expand the zone for my pitcher, and the umpire doesn't even realize it.

Swaying

I bring up swaying again at this point in the chapter because it is directly involved with the umpire. I sway to the left with my body when I am catching a pitch to the left of me. I sway to the right with my body when I am catching a pitch to the right of me. The key to swaying is keeping my shoulders squared up to the pitcher, never letting my body become tilted to the left or the right when catching a pitch. I will put myself in a strong position to catch the baseball.

There is, however, such a thing as swaying too much and obstructing the view of the umpire. I know as a catcher that with a right-handed hitter at the plate, the umpire will be over my left shoulder. When the umpire is over my left shoulder, I can only sway three to four inches at the most to the left — any more than that and I may take away his view of the pitch. As far as shifting to the right when the umpire is over my left shoulder, I can sway as much as needed. (With a left-handed hitter everything is exactly the opposite.) One more thing to consider is that since every umpire sets up differently, it is up to me to talk to the umpire. I need to ask him to let me know if I am in any way obstructing his view when I am swaying. If I am, then I need to make an adjustment. After all, he is the one calling the balls and strikes

In wrapping up the receiving part of this chapter, keep a few things in mind. First, receiving, for most catchers, is an acquired skill; they must work on it daily throughout the course of their careers to improve. The best place to work on receiving skills is in the bullpen. Too often, young catchers take for granted the time spent catching pitchers in the bullpen, which is a great place to perfect every aspect of receiving. A young catcher should beg and plead to catch in the bullpen everyday in order to work on his receiving skills. Remember, it's not enough just to catch the ball; a good, hard-working catcher will receive each pitch with a purpose and try to look good while doing so.

Blocking

Blocking is a different beast altogether. A catcher can have the most perfect blocking mechanics in the world but if he doesn't have that "get down-and-dirty, warrior mentality," he will be average at best at blocking. Sherlock used to say to me, "We have to be tough S.O.B.'s and d---s in the dirt." In other words, block everything, relying on mental and physical toughness to do so.

Second only to receiving, blocking is an extremely important aspect of catching, and I think there are four reasons—some obvious and some perhaps not so obvious—why a catcher needs to become an effective blocker. (1) I must keep baserunners from advancing on the base paths. (2) With no one on base and two strikes on the hitter, if I fail to block the third strike, the batter might reach first base. (3) If a pitcher, who is letting up on his curveball or slider because he is worried about my ability is to block it, then he becomes a less effective pitcher. (4) Protecting the umpires. If in every game I miss blocking seven or eight baseballs, chances are that the umpire will be struck by at least one of them. Not only might he become a little bit skittish behind the plate, but also he could, subconsciously, be less apt to give me that pitch just off the corner.

When blocking, the initial stance is critical. As I mentioned earlier in this chapter, the ready stance with my throwing hand behind my glove is what I will use when I am blocking. From this ready stance, I am in the good position to block just about any ball thrown to me. Once I recognize that the ball is in the dirt, I start by falling forward, driving my knees straight down into the ground. I never—*never*—retreat or move backwards with my knees. If I retreat while I am blocking, there is a higher chance of the ball taking a bad hop and skipping to either side of me. (The theory is the same as an infielder's trying to get the

The ideal blocking position: head down, chest forward, glove on the ground.

short hop.) I can then put my glove (with the throwing hand behind) on the ground between my legs. Make sure the glove is on the ground; I don't want any baseballs scooting through my legs just because I don't get my glove all the way down.

At this point my arms will be along the side of my body, keeping as much of my chest exposed as possible — after all, the chest is the area of the body I want to use to block the ball. The chest will be angled slightly down in order to keep the ball directly in front of me. My head is tucked down to protect my throat. When blocking balls to my left or right, I want to angle my body slightly towards the plate in order to keep the blocked baseball as close to the middle of the diamond as possible. If can do that, it will allow me to recover the baseball quickly, while putting me in a good position on the field for possible throwing situations. When blocking to the right, I take my right leg and *throw* it out to the right. This technique will allow me both to get me to the ideal blocking position, and to help me achieve the angle I need (with my chest square to the shortstop) to keep the ball in the middle of the field. When blocking to the left, I simply throw my left leg out to the left side, keeping my chest square to the second baseman.

Throwing the right leg out to get the body in the proper position to block a pitch far to the right of the catcher.

Throwing the left leg out to get the body in the proper position to block a pitch far to the left of the catcher.

On final point about blocking: exhale. As I am about to absorb the baseball's impact, it helps me to exhale. When I expel the air from my chest, I will deaden the impact of the ball, keeping the ball even closer to me in a throwing situation. It's tough to do, especially since my first reaction when blocking is to tense up. However, I still need to stay relaxed in order to soften the body.

Throwing

Even though I have put throwing at the end in the order of importance list, it is the aspect of catching I enjoy the most (and the one aspect of catching most highly scrutinized by scouts). To me, there is nothing better then watching the would-be base stealer walk with his head down back to the dugout. Whether a catcher has a great arm or an average arm, he can improve his "pop-time" to second base through proper mechanics. (Pop-time is the time that elapses from when the pitch hits the catcher's glove to when the throw hits the second baseman's or shortstop's glove. For the record, the average major league pop time, in a game situation, is 2.00 seconds.)

Throwing out a runner attempting to steal second requires a lot more than just a strong arm, and two main factors are beyond your control. First, the pitcher has to have a decent time to the plate, usually 1.3 seconds or less. (From the time the pitcher, in the stretch, lifts his leg to deliver the ball to the plate to when the ball strikes the catcher's mitt is the pitcher's "delivery time.") There are times when no matter how quickly I get the baseball down to second, if the pitcher has taken too long to get rid of the ball, I have no chance. Further complicating matters is the location of the pitch, *i.e.*, the pitcher has to give me a good throw to the plate, one I can handle. If the pitcher does his job with both the delivery time and the location, then it is up to me to get rid of the baseball quickly with an accurate throw to second base. And remember, all this is supposed to happen in roughly 2.0 seconds or less.

In order to be consistent with my throws — both quickly and accurately — I need to have good mechanics. Through proper mechanics alone, a catcher can take .1, .2, or even .3 seconds off his "pop time." Like blocking, the initial stance when throwing is crucial. I must be in the ready stance with my hand behind the glove. Once again, I am in an athletic position and able to throw to any base I need to. Now I am ready to focus on the ball being pitched. As soon as the pitcher starts his motion and I can see that the runner is heading to second, I have to

Receiving the ball in the ready position, preparing to throw to second base.

"get something going," and the trigger is the left leg (assuming again that all catchers are right-handed).

Before the baseball reaches me, I have to tuck my left leg in slightly so I can get my weight shifted. This weight shift to the left leg will then allow me to take a short step with my right leg. (Note that this slight movement with my leg does not affect the upper portion of the body. When the leg-tuck takes place, I have to keep the shoulders squared up to the pitcher. I will still be in a good position to catch every pitch without being susceptible to the baseball thrown on my left side.)

While all this is going on with my lower half, I can't simply forget about the upper half, which has its own technique. As I am about to take a short step with my right foot, I must have a quick, clean exchange from my glove to the throwing hand. If you remember the "receiving" section, I mentioned how crucial it is to let the ball come to me, as opposed to stabbing at it. It's a case of simple logic: the pitched ball can travel faster than my arm can bring the ball back to me. (The same theory holds true for an infielder receiving a throw from the catcher at second base on a steal. He must let the travel all the way to the base instead of reaching out and bringing the ball back to the base.) Every *hundreth* of a second counts.

The feet and shoulders have rotated from the ready position as the body rises up to throw.

Once I have caught the ball, it is important that I do not carry the glove with me when I am trying to make the exchange. Instead, I want to keep the glove in the center of my chest throughout the entire transfer. I then just rotate the glove 90° to the right and take my throwing hand to the ball. From here I start the short throwing motion with the throwing arm. It is important to use a short throwing motion here because quickness is of utmost importance. Certainly, a big throwing motion, like that of a pitcher, would provide adequate arm strength, but it would sacrifice too much quickness and would expend valuable time.

With pitches thrown to the left, I take the glove to the ball and "rake" it back into the center of the chest, where the transfer takes place. Pitches to the right, however, are a little bit different. Instead of raking the ball back into the chest for the transfer, I just rotate my shoulders and take my throwing hand to the ball. The pitch to the right already puts me in a good throwing position, since the transfer naturally takes place on the throwing-hand side. Once the transfer has taken place, I am now ready for the short step with my right foot.

When stepping with the right foot, I have to make sure I am stepping in a straight line to second base. If I were to draw a line directly from second base to the center of my body, no matter where I catch the ball in relation to home plate, my step should be three to five inches in front of me and on this line. Notice that I always refer to the step as a "short" step. With a short step, I can cut down on the time on my throw, not to mention that the short step will keep me out of the way of the

The throwing position: feet and shoulders aiming at second base; arm up; hand on top of the baseball.

hitter. I see a lot of young catchers, when throwing to second base, practically jumping toward second base with their step. Somewhere along the way, someone has told them that in order to attain a strong throw, they must take a huge step toward second to get their momentum going. I strongly disagree. I must take a short step, which in turn will keep the weight on my back leg. I have to get the weight on my backside in order to make a strong throw. Once in this position, I have the baseball in my throwing hand, my weight is back, and my shoulders have to be lined up towards second base.

In this position, I am now ready to throw to second base. It is very important, as more of a mental note than a physical one, to throw *through* the base not just to it. Like hitting through the ball — as opposed to simply making contact and stopping — this mental approach will give me more carry on my throw and thus avoid short-hopping the infielders. Finally, a proper follow-through is critical. Instead of throwing and recoiling, my right leg will come around just after I release the ball (similar to the follow-through of a pitcher), and I will be bent over at the waist.

In throwing to first or third base, I apply the same principals. My footwork is the same except for the direction of my step. Obviously, the short step now goes in the direction of the appropriate base, keeping in mind that the shoulders again have to be lined up to the base.

Throwing to the bases is, in my opinion, the best part of catching. The key to throwing is a quick release and an accurate throw. Too often

I see catchers with great arms but only average "pop" times when throwing to the bases. Any catcher can attain a quicker "pop" time with sound technique and lots of practice.

Some final points

Pop-Ups

For most catchers, there is nothing more difficult than catching a high pop-up directly above him. Through proper technique and practice, however, any catcher can make it look easy. The first step, as you would assume, is to take off the mask and find the baseball. Once I have found the baseball, I have to turn around and face away from the field. Due to the spin on the baseball — which will cause *all* pop-ups to sail towards the pitcher's mound — I must stay "behind the ball" and allow it to come back to me. I now must decide in which direction I need to go in order to catch the baseball. Now that I have determined where the ball is likely to land, I am now ready to discard the mask. I always toss the mask in the opposite direction in which I am moving to catch the ball in order to avoid tripping over it throughout the play.

Here are a couple of hints that will help you with pop-ups. When dealing with pop-ups that are close to the fence, I always find the fence first. Once I find or touch the fence, I can then back up and make the play on the baseball. When I quickly find out where the fence is, I no longer fear crashing into it. Also, do not panic. Try to stay as relaxed as possible during the whole process in order to avoid running around in a state of confusion. Finally, I try to run on my toes as opposed to heel to toe. In doing so, I will be able to keep my eyes steady and prevent the baseball from the appearance of jumping around.

Fielding Bunts

Believe it or not, there is even a technique for fielding bunts. (Unless otherwise noted, all bunts will be thrown to first base). When a catcher fields a bunt, it should result in an easy out, but improper mechanics can lead to disaster. In dealing with the bunt down the first base line — and with all bunts — the first and most important step is to get to the ball as quickly as possible. Once I reach the ball, I must bend *at the legs*, not at the waist in order to stay in a balanced position throughout the play. In retrieving the ball, I must use both the glove and the throwing hand to scoop up the ball. When scooping, I must have my body positioned so that the baseball is directly in the middle or towards the right side of my body, allowing me to keep weight on my backside and in a good position to throw. With my shoulders lined up with first base, I now take a short crow hop with my feet to get my momentum going towards first base and deliver the ball.

The bunt toward the middle of the field is somewhat different. In order to get my shoulders lined up to first base, I have to take a "banana route" to the ball. (This "banana route," both in theory and technique, is similar to that of an infielder when fielding a ground ball.) I start the banana route by shooting out to the left of the baseball and scooping it up in the same manner as the bunt down the first base line. Now, my momentum is going towards first base in order to make a stronger, more accurate throw. (On a side note, if I am throwing to second base on a bunted ball to the middle of the field, I do not need to take a banana route to the ball, as my shoulders will already be lined up properly.)

The bunt down the third base line can also be approached in this same manner when throwing to first; however, I do have to take a little wider route. But there is an alternative technique on this bunt that I prefer called the "reverse pivot." Instead of taking the "banana route," I take a direct route to the right side of the baseball. When I stop over the baseball, it should be in the area of my right foot, expediting the process of getting myself into a good throwing position. I then bend at the knees, not the back, to pick up the baseball with my throwing hand only. (If I have time, I can use both the glove and throwing hand to scoop up the baseball, but for the most part, I will be pressed for time.) From here I make a reverse pivot on my right foot, with my back towards the field, and I keep my weight on the backside and make the throw to first. This technique is a little bit more difficult at first, but it can easily be mastered with practice. It is very effective when dealing with well-placed bunts down the third base line.

Dealing with Umpires

Getting along with umpires can be a little bit tricky, but oftentimes, the success of a team can hinge on its relationship with the "boys in blue." As a catcher, I need to foster a positive opinion of me — and, therefore, of my team — in the home plate umpire's mind. If I can establish a healthy rapport with the umpire, I may be able to steal a few extra strikes for my pitcher or pitchers over the course of the game. Furthermore, there is a good chance while I am up to bat, the umpire may give me a few close pitches in my favor.

To start with, before you even walk onto the field, it is a good idea to know the home plate umpire's name. Umpires don't like to be called "Mr. Umpire" or "Blue." If you know his name before you walk onto the field, it shows a certain respect that is instantly appreciated. Also, don't be afraid to introduce yourself to him: "Hi. I'm Josh. What's your name?"

The next hurdle is arguing balls and strikes. Seldom, if ever, does an umpire like to be told he was wrong about a call. However, it is a catcher's job to work for the pitchers. I must try to get as many strikes called in my team's favor as possible, and I have found that it is best to let a couple of innings go by before I start talking to the umpire about the strike zone. First, I have to learn the parameters of each umpire's strike zone before I can even think about having a legitimate argument. After a few innings, when I feel I have a better idea of his strike zone, I can now question some of his calls if necessary. I like to start every argument with a suggestion. For example, "That looked darn good. Can you give us another look at that pitch?" Another example might be, "We cannot throw it right down the middle all day. You are going to have to start giving us some of those corners." These are just two suggestions that you can use to start conversations about the strike zone.

The key when working with umpires it to treat them with respect. Like ballplayers, umpires have large egos, and any disrespecting of them can negatively affect the calls they make for you. Never show up an umpire by turning around after a bad call. Also, holding a strike that the umpire has called a ball is another way of showing him up. Remember, an umpire's sole purpose is to have the game run as smoothly as possible and to get it over with. If a catcher can show the umpire that he is there to help in this cause, it can only work in the catcher's favor.

Plays at the Plate

A play at the plate can be one of the most dangerous aspects of the game. Proper mechanics on this play is critical, not only for keeping a run from scoring but also for our safety as well. A catcher knows he must "block the plate," but how does he do this effectively while keeping out of harm's way?

The first step is to keep the mask on during a play at the plate. Doing so assures my safety and will help out with my confidence level when holding my ground with a two hundred-pound (or more) runner bearing down on me. If a catcher is not used to leaving the mask on during plays at the plate, he should practice taking ground balls — receiving fungoes hit by a coach — at the plate with it on.

Setting up to block the plate. Notice the left shin guard pointing directly at the runner.

Getting as low as possible when applying the tag and using two hands.

"Rolling" with the runner to deflect the force of impact at the plate.

Next is footwork. Depending upon from which direction the ball is being thrown — left field, centerfield, or right field — I have to square my body up in that direction. My body will be bent at the knees, similar to an infielder. I am now in a good, athletic position to catch any throw, especially the dreaded short-hop. Remember that the lower I get, the better position I am in to absorb the blow. Now, and this is very important, I have to take my left foot and place the heel on the corner of the plate that is facing towards third base, and I have to point my left foot directly at the runner rounding third base. The latter point is essential for two reasons. The first reason is that now, I have my shin guard facing the runner, which helps me block the plate. Secondly, if I fail to point my toe towards the runner, my knee will be exposed on the side, leaving me in a vulnerable position. By facing the front of my knee towards the incoming runner, my knee is in a stronger position to take a hit.

Once I catch the ball, if I have time, I grab the ball with both hands to avoid dropping the ball on impact. Next I have to make an aggressive tag by using the "roll" method. By rolling to the left as I make the tag, I will avoid a major collision at the plate and put myself in a good position to make any other plays out on the field. Remember, a good, tough-minded catcher will say, "This is my plate, and I have to protect it." The opposing team is trying to score, and it is the catcher's job to make it as difficult as possible. Sometimes, major collisions are unavoidable and you will end up on your back; that's just part of wearing the "tools of igno-rance."

Becoming a quality catcher requires equal amounts of mental forti-tude, physical toughness, sound technique, and a keen perception of pitchers' psyches. Most of all, though, it requires effort. You must be willing to catch thousands upon thousands of pitches in the bullpen to perfect your

Find the other baserunners after a tag play at the plate.

receiving blocking skills. You must learn how to throw quickly and accu-rately. And you must develop a take-charge, never-say-die attitude. Some baseball people say that the fastest way to the big leagues is by wearing the tools of ignorance. The question is, Do you have what it takes?

5

Baserunning

A few years ago, I asked a 16-year-old baseball player what the five "tools" are. He answered, "Hitting for average, hitting for power, fielding, throwing, and, I don't know, baserunning?" I asked him, "Do you mean foot speed?" He said, "No. Our coach is always telling us how important baserunning is." I just chuckled. You see, a scout couldn't care less how well a player runs the bases. He may get a great primary lead, get a great secondary lead, take perfect angles, and hit each base in perfect stride, but if he is slower than a seven-year itch, no one cares. Scouts are interested in raw speed, and I doubt any player was ever drafted because he was an intelligent baserunner.

Ah, but baserunning is just another facet of baseball that, when addressed properly, can help you in your pursuit of professional baseball. Here's what I mean. Say you're a college senior, and although you have only average footspeed, you scored 80 runs in 60 games. The scout who has followed you all year is speaking to his boss, the Scouting Director. The scout says, "You know, this kid doesn't run all that great, but he goes first third all the time, I never saw him get thrown out at home when trying to score from second on a two-out single, and somehow, he scored 80 runs (which seems "more" than 79). He must be doing something right." Furthermore, by focusing on good leads and proper angles, you may able to score five or six more runs per year, which could mean the difference between leading the conference in runs scored or finishing fourth.

Also, baserunning is the one phase of the game that can be improved, as a team, by simply paying attention to details. Look, no manager will ever get on your case for failing to score from first base on a double if you read the ball correctly and make good turns around the bases. The lack of speed that prevents you from scoring is something that he can't teach you. Few things, however, irk a manager more than baserunning mistakes because all baserunning errors are mental. Failure to tag up on fly ball from second base with nobody out, being picked off at first base on a failed bunt attempt, and being doubled off on a line drive to the shortstop are just a few examples of "brain cramps" on the basepaths. Not only will you incur the wrath of your manager, but also you will prevent your team from scoring a valuable run or two.

Angles

Until I reached professional baseball, every amateur coach I had talked about taking the "question mark" route to first base. What these coaches meant is that the runner, on a single to the outfield, should run directly on the baseline until about 15–20 feet before first base. At that point, he should veer out to the right for a few steps, and then turn back into the field of play by touching first base with at a perpendicular angle to the first-base line. In pro ball, though, all the coaches I ever had taught the technique in a different way.

First, after making contact with the ball, find out where it's going. In other words, make sure that the ball will make it through the infield. If you start your turn prematurely and the infielder makes a highlight-reel play, he may be able to throw you out at first base because you will have lost valuable steps. (This nearly happened to me once. I hit a ball sharply up the middle, and figuring that the shortstop would never get to the ball, I started thinking about rounding first base. Unfortunately, the shortstop dove for the ball, popped up, and threw to first base. Luckily, I beat the throw by barely a step, but the play shouldn't have been nearly as close.)

I would guess that nine times out of ten, you will know when the ball hits the bat whether or not the ball is in its way to the outfield. Assuming that the ball is destined for the outfield, you should start your sprint to first base by running right at the coach's box. At roughly 60–75 feet down the line, you will begin to angle back into the field of play, trying to step on first base on a path as close to parallel as possible to the 1st–2nd baseline. Notice that you will hit the base in the exact same position as you will in the question-mark technique, but in my opinion, the latter technique will allow you to be running faster when touching the base. Certainly, the amount of distance between the baseline and the runner's path — and also the point at which the runner will start his turn back into the field — is based on the agility of each runner.

The same techniques apply when approaching both second and third base. Once you have determined that there will be no force or tag play at the upcoming base, you must get as wide as you can *as quickly as you can.* Doing so will give you both the angle and momentum needed to advance to the next base if desired. Bill Plummer told me about the second base-man from the Big Red Machine days, Joe Morgan. He said Morgan, who was quite a quick little baserunner, came as close to making perfect, 90° turns as anyone he ever saw. As a two-time NL MVP, Morgan scored a ton of runs for his team, and you can be sure that his ability to round the bases with near-perfect precision helped him score a few more runs each year.

SBD: *s*igns, (score)*b*oard, *d*efense

So, you've reached first base, come back to the bag, and given your batting gloves to the first base coach. Immediately, you must find the third base coach and receive the signs. There is nothing a third base coach hates more that having to wait for a baserunner to look at him, especially when the baserunner is chatting with the first baseman or the first base coach. Most third base coaches want to give their signs as quickly as possible to prevent the other team from focusing on them and stealing their signs.

Next, you have to know the situation of the game, and if it helps, look at the scoreboard. You need to know how many outs there, what the count is, and what inning you're in. With one out, your thought process of approaching second base will be vastly different from that of two outs. If you have a chance to advance from first to third on a hit and you don't because of not knowing how many outs there are, you could cost your team a scoring opportunity — and receive a good tongue-lashing in the process.

Finally, you must look at the positioning of the defense. Certainly, a left fielder will play a big, right-handed hitting pull hitter differently from a small, left-handed hitting slap hitter. Knowing where each defender is at the crack of the bat will help you take the extra base — or keep you at the current base — if the situation presents itself.

Leads from first base

Primary Lead

It's a myth to think that the size of your primary lead depends on your foot speed. Regardless of how fast you are, you need to find out,

Leading off first in front of baseline puts the runner too close to both the first baseman's and the middle infielder's glove on a tag play at either first or second base.

as early in your career as possible, the maximum lead you can take without being picked off. For the umpteenth time, every step counts, especially when you are slow and can't afford any wasted ones. That extra eight inches of primary lead may mean the difference between an "out" or "safe" call on a force play at second base, and the result of that call can directly alter the outcome of the game. Furthermore, if a scout in the stands sees you get called out on that play, it could also affect his opinion of you. Remember, every little bit counts.

There are two schools of thought on primary leads (also known as lead-offs) from first base. First, draw an imaginary line from the geometric center of first base to the geometric center of second base (we'll call this the baseline). Some coaches like their runners to lead off in front of this line to create an optical illusion for the pitcher. When standing eight to twelve inches in front of the baseline, a runner appears to be closer to the base than if he were standing directly on the baseline. If the pitcher doesn't recognize this deception, the runner may gain an extra half-step in his route to second base. I suppose this type of lead is acceptable, but there is one downside: the runner is farther away from the back corners of both first and second base. In other words, if, on a pickoff attempt, a runner is trying to reach the back corner of first base — the farthest point away from the pitcher — with his right hand, his dive back to the base will take longer (due to the lengthening of the hypotenuse of the imaginary triangle).

The other line of thinking is to stand eight to twelve inches behind the baseline. From this position, the runner can dive directly at the back corner of first base, and, if stealing, he will be in line with the back corner of second base. In both instances, he will make contact with the base

Leading off first base behind the base-line, perhaps a bit too far, but better than being in front of the basline.

at the farthest point away from where the throw originates. The other benefit of starting in this position is that when trying to go from first base to third base, you will find yourself more able to make a sharp turn around second base. Personally, as someone who was never a stolen base threat, I preferred the latter lead. It was more important for me to be able to go first to third than to try to steal second. Like most facets of baseball, experiment with each one to find out what works for you.

Once you have gone through the SBD procession, you are now ready to leave the base. Like hitting, pitching, and fielding, doing the same thing over and over again is crucial. You need to duplicate the same steps—literally—each time to determine how far off the base you can go. Starting with both feet on the base, face second base and take a large step with your right foot first, then with your left foot, and then with your right foot again. Just before your right foot hits the ground, start to pivot on your left foot so when your right foot lands, your shoulders are parallel to the baseline. This is the basic lead for all baserunners.

From here, depending on the pickoff move of the pitcher and your intentions as a baserunner, you now begin to take tiny shuffle steps towards second base until you've reached your maximum, safe distance. Again, it is important that you teach your mind this distance because you cannot look down at your feet or rely on the cut of the grass to help you. Looking down at your feet could result in a pickoff, and each field is manicured differently. You must use the consistency of your steps to figure out where your lead should be.

The last part of primary leads has to do with one-way and two-way leads. If you are not a consistent threat to steal bases, then you should *never* be picked off. You will take a one-way lead, which means that you will get a large yet safe primary lead with your body weight slightly towards first base. Then, once the pitcher picks up his front leg and begins his delivery, you proceed into your secondary lead with two hard "shuffle" steps. The idea is to land on your right foot in your second shuffle step at the moment the hitter would make contact with the ball. Obviously, you don't want to be too committed to second base that you can't return to first base quickly. Again, it better to err on the side of caution; not too many things incense a manager more than watching one of his runners being picked off by a catcher.

As a base stealer, there is an inherent risk in the large primary lead required to steal second base. Not only do you have to be aggressive in your primary lead to shorten the distance to second base but also you have to be ready to take off with the first flinch of the pitcher. Both of these factors can lead to being picked off. The base stealer needs to have a two-way lead, meaning he has to be able to go right or left with equal effectiveness. Regardless, he will be picked off from time to time, and a coach has to be able to accept the bad — being picked off — with the good — a successfully stolen base.

Two Thoughts

When you are getting your primary lead, *never* take your eyes off the pitcher. Chuck Hartman, my coach at Virginia Tech, used to say, "The bases haven't moved in 100 years." What he meant was that there is no need to look at first base while you are taking your lead. In the split-second it takes you shift your eyes from the pitcher to first base and back to the pitcher, he might initiate his pickoff move and catch you. Learn your own personal lead and footwork so you will know exactly how far off the base you are in your primary lead.

Secondly, in a 3–2 count, two-out situation, you will be "running with the pitch." In other words, when the pitcher picks up his leg, you will take off. Most of the time, the first baseman will be playing behind you in order to increase his range, so there is no fear of being picked off. (If he does try to sneak behind you for a "back-door" pickoff, it is up to your first base coach to alert you.) Now, knowing that there will be virtually no chance of a force play at second base — you will be too close to the base since you will be running with the pitch — wouldn't it make sense to start thinking about third base? You bet. As you'll see when I discuss leads at second base, you should get your primary lead about three feet behind the baseline and approach second base on a line parallel to the baseline. While this angle may make you a step or two

Taking first step on primary lead from first base, eyes on the pitcher.

Taking second step on primary lead from first base, eyes on the pitcher.

Leading off at first base, eyes on the pitcher.

slower to second base, it will make you three or four steps faster overall to third base. Just one more thing to consider.

Secondary Leads

The secondary lead from first base is more important than the primary. I see it happen all the time: a kid will get a huge primary lead only
to take a timid secondary lead in fear of being picked off. He doesn't
have his momentum going towards second base at contact, and he
doesn't explode as quickly as he could have. It is better to shorten the
primary lead and have a more explosive secondary lead. Think about it
logically. Let's say that in both examples, you right foot lands on a spot
20 feet from first base. In the first instance, you land on the spot with
body almost still. In the second case, though, you land with your
momentum leaning towards second base. You will be able to fire out to
second base better in the latter example.

One of the big keys to a quality secondary lead is keep your knees
bent and your feet as close to the ground as possible (in other words,
don't hop; shuffle). You must also keep your weight as close to the vertical centerline of your body as you can. If your weight shifts too dras-
tically to one side of the body or the other, you may find yourself off

balance and unable to move effectively in a certain direction. Like the primary lead, you must know the maximum distance from first base you can be without being picked off by the catcher (knowing his arm strength and his proclivity to throw to first base *beforehand* would help, don't you think?).

Lefties

While right-handed pitchers rely on quickness in their pickoff moves, lefties use deception. Getting a comfortable lead with a left-handed pitcher on the hill can be quite difficult. Even more difficult is leading off against a lefty with an outstanding pickoff move. If you and your team come across this type of pitcher, there is not a whole you can do about it. You have say, "Look, if I try to take my conventional lead against this guy, he's gonna pick me off. I need to accept that he has a great pickoff move and just try to counteract it the best I can."

When I was with the High Desert Mavericks in 1997, we had a lefty, Chris Michalik, on our staff. I played first base for the second half of the year, and in that *half*-season, he must have picked off 10 baserunners. Heck, he wasn't even a starter, just a middle reliever, meaning that he had fewer chances to pick off runners, and he still caught a guy every second or third outing. His move was exceptional, and even as a first baseman who saw him from the same angle each time he pitched, I had no idea where the ball was going until he released it. (Incidentally, Michalik later became a starting pitcher for the Toronto Blue Jays, and I heard ESPN analyst Peter Gammons say that he had the best pickoff in the major leagues. I wanted to say to the TV, "Thanks, Pete, but tell me something I don't know.")

Against a pickoff move of this caliber, you *cannot* be picked off. You must get a one- or two-step lead at the most and wait until you know *for sure* that ball is on its way to home plate. Once you see the ball leave his hand, then you must shuffle off the base as rapidly and as far as you can to make up for your minuscule primary lead. You simply have no choice but to concede to his move (remember my observation about lefties with good pickoff moves in the pitching chapter?).

Firing Out Low?

At some point in your career, you have probably had at least one coach tell you to "fire out low." He wanted you to explode out of your secondary lead low because standing up is slower. I have actually seen coaches hold a bat horizontally over the base line about six or eight feet from the base runner, making him "stay low" when taking off. Well, have you ever watched the 100-meter dash in a track-and-field competition? One goal, perhaps the main goal, for each sprinter is to reach his maximum speed as soon as possible. Again, think logically: can you run faster bent over (firing out low) or while in an upright position? If a sprinter could run faster while staying low, then he would stay in that position for the duration of the race. I have never seen a sprinter run while hunched over. The key for the sprinter is to get to his ideal running form immediately. The same concept holds true for a base stealer. Get your chest up and get going.

Leads from second base

Now that you've reached second base and are in scoring position, it is imperative that you do everything you can to score. There are few things more debilitating to a team than watching a runner at second being thrown out at home plate, especially with two outs. The angle you take when approaching third base is directly related to how fast you can make it to home plate.

Primary Leads

Due to the blind spot that exists naturally when leading off second base, you must rely on your third base coach to help you. Each coach will have his own words or phrases to let you where the shortstop and second baseman are. Like leading off at first base, it is imperative that you keep your eyes on the pitcher the entire time. Until you get the playoffs in the big leagues, there should be no problem in hearing your coach. Therefore, by opening your ears to him and your eyes to the pitcher, you should be able — assuming you and your coach are on the same page — to make it back to second base every time on a pickoff attempt.

There are basically two types of primary leads from second base: the in-the-baseline lead and the behind-the-baseline lead. As a base stealer, you will be in the baseline most of the time, as you will be as close to third base as possible. Also, in bunt situations, you need to be in the baseline for the same reason.

If you are not a speed guy, you will take the vast majority of your leads in the "two-out" primary lead position. To get to this position, you want take roughly two large steps off the base in the baseline and two regular steps perpendicular and back from the baseline. You will be at a better angle for rounding third base, and like going first to third, the ability to get to third base is less important than the ability to get to home. Again, if you are not a base stealer, you *cannot* be picked off, for any reason. The first time I was ever picked off at second base, my coach told me, "Get your lead with your secondary," meaning that a shorter primary lead with a long and powerful secondary lead is ideal.

Secondary Leads

During my junior year of college, I heard a coach say something I have never forgotten. I was playing third base, and in a bunt situation, he yelled to his runner at second base, "You can't get here [he pointed to third base] unless he [he pointed to the hitter] does his job." I see it happen all the time: the runner at second base tries to get such a big lead that if the batter bunts through the ball (doesn't make contact), the catcher throws behind him and picks him off. That should *never* happen.

The same tenets hold true with the secondary lead from second base as they do for first base. You want to time the landing of your right foot with the point of contact by the hitter. As I mentioned, it is usually better to take a shorter primary lead and a longer secondary lead. Doing so will help prevent you from being picked off by the pitcher. Then, as soon as you see the hitter take the pitch or swing through it, take one or two hard steps back towards second base to prevent the catcher from a pickoff attempt.

At Contact

In my opinion, more baserunning errors occur at second base than at the other two combined, and most of the time, the baserunner fails to read the ball off the bat initially. Also, depending on the number of outs, the baserunner's mental approach will vary.

With nobody out, your sole job is to get to third base with less than two outs. Obviously, the batter plays a large role in your ability to get there, and your success hinges on a quick and accurate initial read of the ball off the bat. The general rule states that you, after you've taken your secondary lead, should advance to third base on any ground ball hit directly at you or to your left. Even if you don't run particularly well and even if the ball is hit hard right at you, you can make it to third base with a quick reaction to the ball. The key is to fire out as quickly as possible because most shortstops will be deterred from throwing to third base if they see you make a fast read.

On a fly ball, you must retreat to the base immediately and find out where the ball will land. Knowing the arm strength of the outfielders is critical here, as your decision to run on the medium-distance fly ball is based primarily on this knowledge. On the extremely deep fly ball, even though your instincts are telling you otherwise, you still must retreat to the base. You must be absolutely, positively, 100 percent sure that the outfielder will not catch the ball before you advance off the base. If there is the slightest doubt in your mind, then you must stay on the base and tag up.

With one out, "when in doubt, hang out." Coach Hartman used to say this phrase to us. With one out, if there is the slightest doubt in your mind about whether the outfielder will catch the ball or not, you must "hang out," *i.e.,* wait between second base and third base to see if the outfielder will catch it. If he catches the ball, simply retreat to the base. If he is unable to get to it, you should be able to score easily. How far off the base you venture is dependent upon the following three factors: the depth of the ball in the outfield, the arm strength of the outfielder, and your quickness in returning to the base. As a rule, you should be far enough off the base to make back safely by a step if the outfielder attempts to throw to second base.

Leading off from second base with two outs.

There is one exception to the hang out rule — the extremely deep, yet easily catchable fly ball. Say your big, powerful cleanup hitter just barely misses a homerun and hits a towering fly ball to the leftfielder on the warning track. If you know that the leftfielder is "camped" (waiting for the ball to come down), then you can return to second base and tag up. If, however, you see that the ball is definitely not leaving the park but the leftfielder is still moving back on the ball — or perhaps the wind or sun is affecting his ability to catch the ball — then you must "hang out" in order to score if he drops the ball.

Beware of Interference

I saw a play in a major league game once that made me decide to include this section. Atlanta was playing in Philadelphia, and the Braves were leading 5–4 in the top of the ninth. Vinny Castilla was on second base and another Brave was third base with one out. With the Phillies infield playing in to prevent the runner on third from scoring, the Braves hitter hit a sharp ground ball up the middle. Jimmy Rollins, Philadelphia's shortstop, in an attempt to get to the grounder, collided with Castilla. I'm sure that the collision occurred first by virtue of Rollins's reaction to the ball but moreover because of Rollins's field awareness, which in a split-second told him that Castilla would be charged with interference if contact were made. Indeed, Castilla was charged with interference and called out, the runner on third base who had just scored had to return, and the Braves didn't score that inning. The Phillies, aided by the late-inning heroics of Scott Rolen and Pat Burrell, won the game in extra innings.

Castilla apparently forgot the baserunning rule that states all fielders have right-of-way when attempting to field a ground ball or pop-up. It is up to the baserunner to avoid the fielder, even if the fielder is directly in the baseline. In Castilla's situation, with Rollins standing directly in Castilla's running lane (I could not see if Rollins was standing in the actual baseline), Castilla needed to move either well in front of Rollins or well behind him to avoid a possible collision. Unfortunately for the Braves, he did not make the necessary adjustment, and it cost the Braves the game.

From a personal standpoint, I can relate similar to situations. In pro baseball, where players are more buddy-buddy with their opponents than in the amateur ranks, I would actually ask the shortstop, "Hey, man, are you playing in front or behind the [base]line?" Also, as a runner on first base in a potential bunt situation, I asked the first baseman the same question: "You starting right there?" Whatever it takes, you, as a runner, need to determine where you will take your primary and secondary leads to avoid any interference calls that could hurt your team.

Leads from third base

Primary Lead

As a rule, the farther away from the base the third baseman is, the farther off the base you can be. After all, he is the only one capable of receiving a pickoff throw (unlike second base, where two different fielders can nab you). At first base and second base, I generally recommend a "small primary lead, large secondary lead" approach. At third base, though, it's backwards. Because pitcher-to-third baseman pickoffs are so rare — and so easily detectable — at third base, you can get a larger primary lead. On the other hand, you must beware of the catcher-to-third baseman pickoff. A strong-armed, aggressive catcher can put an end to your run-scoring chances in a hurry if you're not careful.

Third base is the one place where virtually all primary leads are identical, due to the fact stealing home is, for all intents and purposes, not an option; in other words, unless you are a creature who runs on four legs, you probably won't be stealing home. Therefore, at third base, only 90 feet from home plate, even more so than at second, you absolutely, positively *cannot* be picked off, especially by the catcher. Most managers would require open-heart surgery in that event.

Secondary Lead

Your primary lead will depend upon the pitcher's choice of delivery — from the stretch or from the windup. The primary lead will vary, but where you end up in your secondary should not vary at all (unless the scouting report says that the opposition's manager likes for his catcher to make a lot of pickoff throws). Once you have decided where you will start, you must first move into foul territory. If a batted ball strikes you while you are standing out of play, then the result is simply a foul ball. If you are hit while standing inside the line, however, you will be called out. Do not stand too far in foul territory because the farther you move out of the baseline, the farther from home plate you will be.

Next, as the pitcher begins his delivery to the plate, you should start walking. At both first and second base, you should get your secondary lead by shuffling away from the base, but third base is different.

Leading off from third base in foul teritory.

The key to the walking lead is to have your right foot land (with your chest facing home plate as opposed to facing, say, the second baseman) at the precise moment the batter would make contact. If he either takes the pitch or swings and misses, you must immediately turn around a full 180° and sprint back to the base. The most important thing about your retreat is to return in fair territory. That way, if the catcher attempts a pickoff throw to the third baseman, you will be in the catcher's ideal throwing lane. Not only will you make his throw difficult, but also there would be a chance that the throw could hit you, which would allow you scamper home in some instances.

Unlike at second base, at contact, the manager usually predetermines the reads off the bat, and these decisions are based on the situation of the game and his propensity towards or reluctance to aggressiveness. For example, he may tell you to "go on contact" or to go on a "down angle" or to "see the ball through the infield." A lot of the time, advancing from third base is a gamble by the manager, and if you read the ball correctly and do what he has told you to do, no manager worth a grain of salt will ever reprimand you if you are thrown out.

Landing on right foot, weight slightly on front leg, shoulders square to home plate, as the pitch enters the hitting zone.

Returning to third base in fair territory.

Sliding

During my first summer of professional baseball in 1995, in one particular game, the opposition's right fielder attempted to throw me out twice at the plate on hard singles. I was trying to score from second base, and never being much of a speed demon, I arrived at the plate just as the ball did on both plays. Somehow, though, I managed to elude the tag of the catcher with two nifty slides. On one of the plays, I actually slid past the plate and reached back with my left hand and touched the plate while the catcher was trying to tag my legs. I don't know if it was my ability to slide or the catcher's inability to block the plate effectively that allowed me to score. Regardless, I scored in both instances, and on the bench, I received quite a few compliments after the second play. The funny part is this: I had never, *ever* worked on sliding in my life.

Sliding is a facet of the game that no one really practices, not even in pro baseball. Oh, sure, during my three spring trainings in the minors, on three or four different days, the coaches would put out the sliding pad to allow us to work on our slides. For the most part, though, learning how to slide is an instinct that a player develops over many years of playing baseball. Therefore, there is not a whole lot for me to say about sliding, but there are two points I need to address.

When in Doubt, Slide

Pete Rose, that famous headfirst slider, used to say, "Going 'all out' all the time won't get a player hurt, but letting up will." Let me give an example. In 1997, I think, Deion Sanders was attempting to steal third base in a game. He had the base stolen easily, and it appeared that the catcher wasn't even going throw the ball. At the last second, though, he uncorked his throw, and Sanders, who had begun to decelerate, had to speed up at the last second, culminating in an awkward reach for the base with his foot. Well, he landed on the base off-balance and suffered a severely sprained ankle in the process. If he had taken Rose's advice and just gone in and slid hard, that injury might have never happened. You need to play enough games in your baseball career that you learn how to slide properly and pain-free so you will be unafraid to get dirty.

For another example, take Game 3 of the 2001 AL Divisional Playoffs. It was nip-and-tuck game until Jeremy Giambi appeared to be on his way to breaking a scoreless tie late in the game until Derek Jeter came out of nowhere to make a play that will live in October lore forever. He shoveled the ball from the first base line to catcher Jorge Posada, who could not see Giambi bearing down on the plate due to his receiving the ball from Jeter. For some reason, Giambi never slid, and Posada put a last-second tag on him. The Yankees went on to win the game and series. Everyone praised Jeter for the play of a lifetime, but no one seemed to fault Giambi for his decision not to slide, and had he slid, he most likely would have scored.

Slide Intelligently

One rule of sliding says never to slide head-first into home plate. If a catcher blocks the plate effectively, you could end up with a broken finger or a dislocated shoulder or both. I have to disagree with this rule in certain instances. Yes, if the catcher is standing over the plate with the ball in his hand, then simply slide into him feet-first and take your medicine. If, however, he has to jump for the ball, or if he has to go up either baseline to receive the throw, then he will be in no position to block the plate effectively. When the catcher has to leave the plate, then sometimes a headfirst slide is ideal.

Once you've seen where the catcher is going to be when you arrive at the plate and you know *for a fact* that he won't be able to block the plate, then opt for the headfirst slide. For one, it is more accurate. There is no rule that says the runner has to touch a certain amount of the plate. If you make a "back-door" slide and catch just two inches of the plate with the tips of your fingers, then you will be safe. In other words, you can control the direction of your hands better than the direction of your feet. Secondly, you can get lower. A hand flat on the ground is a lot more difficult a target for a catcher to reach than a foot sticking up off the ground. Remember, every little bit helps.

If this book is about anything, it's about controlling what you can control in your life. It takes no talent — none — to learn how to run the bases effectively. I didn't say anything about the speed with which you run the bases; that, after all, is one of the things you cannot control. Taking proper angles around the bases, making quick and accurate reads, and above all, using your head, can all contribute to your success as a baserunner. You don't need to be a speed demon to score your fair share of runs.

In the "Dealing with Coaches" chapter, I will mention how important it is for you to maintain a good rapport with all your coaches because of the tightly knit circle within the profession. Good and bad labels can propagate themselves very quickly. Ideally, if you're not a plus runner, you would like to hear your amateur coach say to a college coach or a scout, "You know, Johnnie doesn't run all that fast, but boy, he takes great angles, and I've never seen him get thrown out trying to take the extra base." If the coach or scout knows that you've paid attention to the finer points of baserunning, then he will probably consider you to a "student of the game," and that label is never a bad one to have attached to you.

6

In the Outfield

I did a baseball camp a few years ago, and at the end of the two days, each instructor had to give a brief summary about the skill he taught. When it was the outfield instructor's turn to speak, he asked, "What's the most important part of being a good outfielder?" The kids then answered, in unison, "Swing the bat!" It was obvious what this instructor, who played for a few years in the minors (and even won a stolen base title in AA one season), was insinuating: an outfielder is only as valuable as his ability to hit the baseball.

It seems that each year, less and less emphasis is placed on defense in baseball. In today's game, if you strike out 120 times and are a liability in the outfield but hit thirty homeruns each year, you can still make a ton of money. Everybody wants power at the plate, and oftentimes, the requisite power comes at the expense of speed and agility, two traits needed to be a quality defensive outfielder. To me, though, you don't need to be especially fast and agile to become an above-average defensive outfielder; like every other chapter in this book, it's based on how bad you want to be good.

I remember reading a story about Ryan Klesko. In the mid–1990s he showed his ability to hit major league pitching and therefore became a focal point of the Atlanta Braves' offense. He had been primarily a first baseman in the minor leagues, but there was a problem: the Braves signed Fred McGriff to be their everyday first baseman. Certainly, McGriff—due to lack of the necessary footspeed and arm strength as well as his status—wasn't about to change positions to accommodate a young player, so Klesko, who throws and bats left-handed, had some soul-searching to do. Knowing that he had proven to be a dangerous hitter at the major league level, he could have stormed into GM John Schuerholz's office and demanded a trade. Rather, he decided to learn to play left field.

In this story, I recall the specific quote, "While my buddies were out fishing all winter, I was shagging flies." I have to believe that Klesko, having tasted the spoils of big league life, wasn't about to return to the minors, and he felt compelled to do whatever was required to stay in the Bigs. In order to stay in the majors—and with the powerhouse Atlanta Braves—he had to learn to play the outfield. He did.

One final note about Klesko. At the beginning of 2002, as a member of the San Diego Padres, he was asked to play left field again to accommodate the Padres' latest "can't-miss-kid," third baseman Sean Burroughs. Actually, incumbent third baseman Phil Nevin had to move to first base, forcing Klesko to the outfield. Regardless, Klesko moved yet again and was able to remain in San Diego, the city to which he decided to move when he became a free agent in 1999.

In the big leagues, where salaries rocket more and more out of control each year, versatility is greeted by general managers with open arms. Think about it. If a player can hit and field his position, he is a valued commodity, but if he can hit and field his position *and* several other positions, he is virtually indispensable. Nowhere in a major league player's contract does it say that the team will pay him more money for each position he plays other than his "official" position. Versatility can keep a fringe player around for a long time.

The hard facts

Playing the outfield certainly requires a certain amount of speed, but not as much as you would think. Basically, the amount of production you bring to the plate from an offensive standpoint is inversely proportional to the amount of ground you will be expected to cover in the outfield, at least at the corner positions (in centerfield, you will expected to cover a lot of ground because it is primarily a defensive position). By offensive production, I mean what you can bring to the plate to help your team score runs. A speed guy, like an Ichiro Suzuki of the Seattle Mariners, brings offensive production to the plate, but his productivity comes from utilizing his incredible speed to produce runs for his team. Usually, but not always, this speed translates into the ability to play an adequate to above average defensive outfield. Typically, though, GMs and managers seek power in the corner outfield positions, and a guy like a Manny Ramirez, who hits the absolute stuffing out of the baseball, will be given a little latitude for shoddy defensive play.

Also, playing the outfield is like bunting: you are expected to do it correctly, and if you don't, you look like an ass. Basically, errors in the outfield are magnified. In other words, while an error in the infield generally results in only one extra base for the baserunner or baserunners, a dropped fly ball or a bad angle to a line drive usually spells disaster.

Don't be a hero

Because playing the outfield is easier than playing the infield, managers expect a lot less from a corner outfielder. (Incidentally, I keep referring to corner outfielders because a certain amount of speed is required to play centerfield — obviously. Again, you can't control how fast you can run, but just about anyone, no matter how slow afoot, can become at least an average outfielder just by working at it). As an outfielder, if you hustle to the ball, field it cleanly, and throw it accurately to the cut-off man, you've done your job.

Problems arise, though, when an outfielder tries to do too much. For example, if you're in right field with two outs and a runner on second and the batter hits a hard ground ball to you, you will *rarely* throw out the runner at the plate. The exception, of course, is if you have an exceptional arm and the runner on second base is a Clydesdale. But what upsets a manager is trying to make a play when there is no play there to make. If, by trying to get the runner at the plate, you overthrow the cut-off man and allow the hitter to advance to second base, your manager will probably give you an earful. All you need to do charge the ball hard, get rid of it quickly, and hit the cut-off man in the head with as much velocity as you are capable of.

Now, there is one exception. If the winning run is trying to score from second base, then you need to air it out. It makes no sense to hit the cut-off man when he will have to relay the ball to home anyway (unless you have a very weak arm). If the third base coach holds up the runner at third and the hitter takes second base on you, it doesn't really make any difference. The winning is on third base; all the other runners are irrelevant. Again, check with your manager to see under what circumstances he wants you to let it fly so there is no gray area between the two of you.

Lazy, lazy, lazy

There is nothing in the world more frustrating to me than apathy, or, more specifically, in-job apathy. If you are being paid to do a job, then it is up to you to do it to the best of your ability *every single day*. It has been my experience that corner outfielders and first baseman are the laziest players on the team from a defensive standpoint, and it really chaps me. Because they are being paid to hit the ball, most of them spend little time trying to improve their defense. Why they don't exhibit better practice habits is beyond me.

When I moved to first base from third base for the second half of the 1997 season in High Desert, I worked my ass off to become better. During BP, when I wasn't hitting or running the bases, I was fielding groundballs, working on my footwork for a 3–6–3 double play, or imploring infielders to throw me balls in the dirt. It's never been my nature to do something halfway, and although I would have rather stayed at third base, it wasn't my decision. Usually, I had to beg a first baseman to receive balls at first base for me when I was playing third base during BP. Most of them, after taking a few handfuls of groundballs, retreat to the outfield to jerk around with the pitchers and outfielders. I understand that fielding groundballs can be somewhat taxing, but catching throws from infielders? Hardly.

I've always said that 75 percent of a first baseman's defensive worth is receiving throws from the infielders. Most of the time a first baseman can simply smother a groundball and flip it to the pitcher to get an out. The ability to dig throws out of the dirt and to use the whole bag (to move your feet all around the base to cover more ground), however, can save your infielders a lot of errors—and your team a lot of unearned runs. For example, in 1999, shortstop Rey Ordoñez of the New York Mets committed only four errors in 154 games. In 2000 and 2001 combined, in a total of 193 games, he committed 16 errors. What happened? Perhaps he just botched a few grounders that he fielded cleanly the year before. Perhaps. But consider who his first baseman was in 1999 — the smooth-fielding, lifelong first baseman John Olerud — versus who it was in 2000 and 2001—converted catcher/third baseman Todd Zeile, who was playing first base for the first time. Certainly, I didn't see all 16 of Ordoñez's errors over those two seasons, but you can bet the ranch that having Olerud there would have saved six or eight of them. What am I getting at? Like any other part of baseball, repetition is the key to improvement and Teile just didn't have the reps that Olerud had.

When I was in the minors, I practiced my fielding at third base *every single day* during BP. If we had four hitting groups, I would take fungoes for at least an entire group, if not longer, and I would take them alone. It used to tick me off when a pitcher or an outfielder would come over to third base and field with me. If a catcher or another infielder did because he was interested in learning how to play a new position, fine. But I used to ask the unwelcome teammates, "Do you have any money? Because time is money, and if you don't have any money, then don't waste my time." I didn't say it exactly like that, but I got the point across. If my attitude was a bit harsh, so be it, but I wasn't out on the field to make friends. After BP, if you want to jerk around, talk about something, fine, but not when I'm trying to get better.

You must take the same initiative in the outfield. Normally, the pitchers shag fly balls during BP, which is necessary, but only if they don't interfere with outfielders who are concerned with making themselves better. Are you one of them? If you are, then ask the pitchers and other players in your area to hang back on the warning track while you are working on reading balls off the bat. (Tell them if they want to work on their outfield skills—for whatever reason—to do so while you are hitting.) Now, you don't have to run around like a maniac and wear yourself out. Spend a group running after fly balls as if it were a game situation and another group simply reading the ball off the bat, taking six or eight hard strides at the angle needed to catch the ball properly.

Finally, you must assume that every ground ball hit to your side of the field will make it to the outfield. Let me explain. I remember a game in which we were leading by one going into the bottom of the ninth. The other team's hitter hit a seemingly innocent three-hopper between first base and second base, and our right fielder assumed that either the first baseman or second baseman was going to catch it. He hung back at his position, only to see the ball take a wicked hop and bounce over the second baseman's head and into right field. The hitter, who very fast and was sprinting with the crack of the bat, rounded first base and decided to try for second. Well, our right fielder, who being lazy, didn't get to the ball in time, and the runner made it to second base safely. I was livid. It takes absolutely no talent—none—to hustle, and his laziness almost cost us the game.

If the right fielder had attacked the ball and assumed that it was going to make it through the infield, then there is no way the hitter would have even *considered* trying for second, let alone attempted it. He would have fielded the ball with the runner two to three steps past the bag. No runner in his right mind, in that situation, would ever try for second. Our guy, though, lollygagged after the ball, and the play nearly resulted in disaster.

Two important skills

There are hugely important two skills needed to become a quality outfielder — the reverse pivot and getting behind the ball — and I saw both skills exemplified on a daily basis as a teenager growing up in the Pittsburgh area. Barry Bonds, who began his career with the Pirates, won seven or eight Gold Gloves as a leftfielder, and one particular play became his trademark. On a ball hit sharply down the left field line, Bonds, a left-handed thrower, would sprint to the ball, catch it, plant his right foot, make a reverse pivot (turn his back to second base for a split-second), and throw directly to second base. He became so proficient at making this play that before long, runners stopped trying to stretch those hits into doubles, and think about the numbers of runs he prevented by becoming so good at this play.

True, Barry Bonds is an exceptional athlete, but it wasn't just his athletic ability that allowed him to make this play time after time; it was his work ethic. I saw an interview with Bonds' former manager Jim Leyland, who said that in spring training every year, Bonds would spend a little time each day practicing his technique. He would take a bucket of balls down the left field line, and one-by-one, he would sprint to the ball from his position, wheel around, and throw to second base. In other words, he didn't learn how to make this play by accident or by lying around hoping to make it. Bonds, who was making oodles of money for his ability to hit the ball, took it upon himself to make himself into a Gold Glove left fielder. He succeeded.

Andy Van Slyke also won multiple Gold Gloves as a centerfielder while with the Pittsburgh Pirates, and he was a master at "getting behind the ball." This technique is absolutely imperative for an outfielder, yet I see very few outfielders who are able to do it effectively. On a routine fly ball to the outfield, Van Slyke would circle around the ball and get at least twenty or thirty feet behind where he thought the ball would land. Then, depending on where he was going to throw the ball, he would begin to run to that base, and he would catch the ball at a full sprint. That sprint, combined with a powerful crow-hop, would allow him to add a lot more velocity to his throws. In fact, I remember watching highlights of him throwing to home plate from centerfield, and he had so much momentum built up that he would often tumble forward after releasing the ball.

Did Van Slyke have a gift, an instinct, for doing this? Perhaps. Did he practice this technique over and over again? You bet. It's simply not good enough just to catch the ball flat-footed, crow-hop, and then make the throw. You will not get nearly as much velocity as you would by getting behind the ball, and you will waste valuable time. Is this technique difficult to learn? Sure it is. But think about this: With the exception of an All-Star game as a 14-year-old, I have never played an inning of outfield in my entire life, yet I can go out there and catch any fly ball hit to me. Catching the ball is easy, but like playing the infield, catching it in a position to be productive after you've caught is paramount. As former Yankee great Tommy Henrich once said, "Catching a fly ball is a pleasure. Knowing what to do with it after you've caught it is a business."

One final point: With both techniques, you don't need a Howitzer for an arm. Heck, if you just *get* to the ball quickly, you can deter runners from trying to take the extra base. If you can learn both techniques, you can scare opposing baserunners. Think about it from a baserunner's standpoint. If you're unsure of an outfielder's arm strength, yet you see him take a perfect angle to the ball, field it cleanly, and prepare himself to get his entire body into his throw, what do you say to yourself? You say, "Boy, I better be careful about trying to take the extra base on this guy." And don't think coaches and scouts won't notice — both the technique executed properly and the one done poorly.

Trust physics

Before I get into the "trust physics" part, I want to explain the drop-step technique because it is directly related to trusting of physics. The drop-step is the initial step an outfielder takes when a ball is hit over his head. If the ball is hit over his glove-side shoulder, he will drop-step with his glove-side foot. If the ball is hit over his throwing-side shoulder, then he will drop-step with that side's foot. (What about the ball hit perfectly over his head? Which way does he drop-step? Because he will be better able to get his glove in the ideal position to catch the ball — with the glove-side elbow pointing straight down as opposed to pointing up with the wrist turned awkwardly to get the palm of the glove facing up — he wants to drop-step with the glove-side foot. To give you a visual, think of Willie Mays' snare, a.k.a. The Catch, in the 1954 World Series, and picture his body's position. It's easier to get that position by drop-stepping with the glove-side foot.)

The idea is to take the proper angle to the ball immediately, and if your initial step is either slow or in the wrong direction, you may be unable to make up the ground. A good drill to practice making the correct read is to have a coach just throw balls over your head, and you can practice making the initial read. Certainly, if your coach is proficient enough with his fungo bat, he can hit you the ball. Regardless, learning how to identify where the ball is going and taking the correct drop-step is extremely important.

As you probably noticed in your brief career, 99 out of 100 line drives — either from a left-handed or a right-handed hitter — that start directly at one of the foul poles will end up going foul. You have to trust physics. Just as a pop-up behind home plate will come back to the field of play, a line-drive hit directly at a corner outfielder will either stay on its path, or it will veer towards the foul line. It will not (again, the side of the plate from the hitter is hitting is irrelevant) veer towards the gap. Knowing this, it would make to sense to take your drop-step accordingly; for rightfielders, the drop-step will take place with the left foot, and for left fielders, it will take place with the right foot.

Any outfielder will tell you that the line-drive hit right at him is the toughest play for him. Most outfielders will say that the first thing you have to do is to freeze because the tendency is to run in on the ball. If the ball is struck well, it may actually carry over your head. The best outfielders that I've seen not only freeze but also they take a quick drop while they are staying in the same place. If the ball is hit hard, they will then be a position to begin their pursuit of it. Simply freezing will not set your feet properly to run after the ball. You freeze while getting your feet ready to sprint after the baseball.

Positioning

In the infield a player usually starts in roughly the same place. If he does move, it will be only a few steps in any direction. In the outfield, though, the degree of variance is much larger. For example, a left fielder will play a small, skinny, slap-hitting, left-handed hitter much differently from big, lumbering, power-hitting, right-handed hitter. Certainly, size isn't always indicative of the type of hitter at the plate, but it's usually a good reference point. As you move up in the baseball world, scouting reports will become more available, and these charts will give you a better idea about where to play certain hitters. In the meantime, you will have to rely on your own judgment and your coach's preferences to determine your positioning.

Along with positioning, backing up bases is another facet of playing the outfield. Once the ball is put into play and it has not been hit to you, you have two choices: you can stand around and watch what's going on or you can go get near the action. As an obvious example, take a ground-ball to right field with a runner on first base and you're the left fielder. You need to sprint over to foul territory behind third base in case the right fielder's throw to third base goes astray. As a less obvious example, take a groundball to right field (again, you're the left fielder) with a runner on second and two outs. The right fielder delivers his throw to home plate, which is cut off by the first baseman, who sees the hitter try to advance to second base. The first baseman wheels and throws to second base, but he overthrows the base. If you're anticipating where you should be, you can be in a position to field the overthrow and prevent further damage.

For a personal example, here's a story about a play in a game in my junior year of college. There was a runner on second with two outs, and the hitter hit a sharp ground ball to the left fielder. As always, I lined up in the proper cut-off position, and our left fielder hit me perfectly with his throw. Knowing that we had no chance to get the runner at the plate and seeing the batter trying to advance to second base, I cut the throw. I then turned and fired to second base, but my throw was off-line, and it went into the right-center field gap. Unfortunately, no one in the outfield was backing up, and the runner scored all the way from second base.

Was the runner's scoring my fault? Absolutely. It was definitely an error on my part. The damage, however, could have been curtailed by a proper back-up. Each coach — each decent coach — should have his own personal plan as to where the outfielders should be to back up bases properly. The reality is, as you will see, that not every coach you play for will take it upon himself to instruct you. The point is that once the ball is put into play and it's not hit at you, there is *somewhere* you can be. Figure it out. You never know who is watching.

7

Strength and Conditioning

Perhaps the most common question I receive today from young players regards strength training. Seriously, can you blame a kid? Home-runs are flying out of ballparks all over America at a record pace seemingly every year, and the men who hit them make an obscene amount of money to do just that. These men, to be sure, are physical specimens, but they are physical specimens with a skill. Don't think for one minute that living in the weight room will guarantee big-time power; the ability to hit homeruns consistently requires a combination of a fluid swing, bat speed, a good mental approach, and, of course, strength.

I remember returning to Virginia Tech for the fall of my junior year and telling a former teammate of mine that I wanted to hit more — a lot more — homeruns. He said matter-of-factly, "Bo, you don't have the swing for it." As a twenty-year-old hell-bent on playing pro ball, I didn't want to hear it. I was going to lift weights and practice my swing until I became a homerun hitter.

Unfortunately, that day never came. I mean if it were that that easy, every fool with bulging muscles would hit homeruns. I hit 13 homeruns in 58 games as a senior in college, but in roughly 2200 career AB's in the minors, I hit only 32 homers. I was always able to hit the ball hard, but for some reason, I was never able to get that perfect combination of swing plane, force of impact, and backspin to hit consistent homeruns. The reason I mention my personal history is to reiterate that a significant increase in your overall body strength does *not* guarantee an increase in your power numbers; however, weight-training, when done properly, will significantly improve your chances of becoming a power hitter — and will keep you healthy.

Weight training

Now, before you sign up at your local health club and run down to your local GNC to stock up on supplements, you have to determine what type of strength program you are ready for. For example, if you're still growing, you might be wise to proceed with caution. I've asked several people — doctors, sports trainers, and personal trainers — about the effects of weight lifting on the growth plates and joints of a growing body, and I can't seem to get a definite answer. Therefore, I would recommend a standard low-weight, high-repetition weight program. By that, I mean doing sets of at least ten repetitions. The lower the weight, the more "reps" you can do. Generally, power lifters do the opposite routine, opting for higher weight and fewer reps. As a baseball player, you definitely do *not* want the build of a power lifter; you want strong, lean muscles, and the low weight-high rep routine is a better way to go.

Just as hitting and pitching are very individualized, so is a weight-training program. No two people have the same tolerance of pain, the same rate of strength increase, and the same amount of recovery time, so listen to your body. One thing I am adamant about is proper technique. It never made any sense to me to cheat in order to give yourself — or worse, your friends — the impression that you are becoming stronger. Furthermore, overloading your muscles and joints with weight to which they're not accustomed can lead to injuries.

To me, strength training must begin with the core muscles, namely the abdominals and the lower back. Trust me when I say that playing through nagging pain in the any of the limbs is difficult; it is virtually impossible to play with lower back pain. The stronger you can make your abdominals, the better support they will provide for your lower back. Baseball is a very rotational sport, and the advantages to having a strong core to maximize performance and to avoid injuries are numerous.

Let's start with the "abs." It seems as though every six months or so, a new abs-strengthening machine appears. I'm sure some of them are worthwhile, but if strong abs are the goal, then a regimen of crunches and leg lifts will suffice quite nicely — no "gimmick" apparatus necessary. Because the abs is a small muscle group, they can be exercised every other day, or even daily, depending on what you're ready for and how you feel. Furthermore, there is little risk of injury, so you can "burn" your abs as much as you want. At the end of the workout, be sure to stretch your abs properly. The best way to do so is to lie flat on the floor, facedown, and then slowly push yourself up while keeping your hips against the floor. Do it slowly, and hold the position for 8–10 seconds.

The best exercise for the lower back is the reverse extension, which can be done on the "Roman Chair." The idea is to lie facedown on an elevated, padded surface and have someone hold down your legs while you put your hands behind your head and go down towards the floor and back up. Do the exercise slowly, pausing for a second at the top of each rep. I would recommend three sets of 10–12 reps, three days a week.

To me, the legs are the next most important muscle group. For years, the squat has been the granddaddy of all weight lifting exercises, but it has been my experience that it is also one that is often performed improperly. Therefore, I recommend the leg press machine, which will work the same basic muscles but with a much lesser chance of injury. Other good exercises for the legs are leg extensions and leg curls for the upper leg and calf raises for the lower leg. A good "legs" workout will take a lot out of you physically. I can recall that, during one particular offseason, I found it difficult to walk up the steps to my apartment after certain "leg days." If your leg workouts are of similar intensity, I would recommend three or four days of rest before the next leg day. As a rule, the larger the muscle group, the more recovery time needed between days. The legs are obviously a large muscle group — perhaps the largest — so if you really "burn" your legs on a Monday, it would be advantageous to wait until Friday, or even Saturday, to exercise them again.

I would guess that 60–70 percent of injuries in baseball occur in the legs, and I suppose the culprit is inflexibility. Unlike the chest, which we'll move to next, I don't think the legs can be too strong. Whether you're pitching or hitting, the power comes from the legs. However, I cannot stress enough how important it is to stretch daily. If the legs can't be too strong, then they can't be too flexible either. Until you can put your hands flat on the floor with your knees locked, then you can improve your flexibility. Until you can go into a full, hockey goalie-style split, then you can improve your flexibility. In other words, the more you lift, the more you must stretch. Everyone knows that Mark McGwire was perhaps the strongest man in baseball, but did you know that he was one of the most flexible, too? In order to execute a fluid swing, a hitter must be flexible and loose. If McGwire didn't stretch properly, he'd lose the fluidity that allowed him to become a top-notch homerun hitter even before he bulked up.

Personally, I feel that the chest receives too much emphasis in baseball because the muscles have no real use. Yes, a well-developed chest is nice to look at, but that's about it. I will say, though, that you must develop the pectorals a little bit to avoid muscle imbalance, a leading cause of injury. Again, baseball players must be fluid and tension-free in their actions, and an unnaturally thick chest can severely impair the ability to execute fluidly the pitching and hitting motions. I'd hate to see a player have a bang-up year with the bat only to return the next year with a choppy swing as a result of extensive weight lifting.

As for the arms, I remember reading an article about Michael Jordan when he was attempting to make it to the major leagues. He talked about seeing the ballplayers in the clubhouse and marveling at the strength in their arms. Jordan had become an avid weight lifter during his years with the Chicago Bulls, but his focus was on the trunk muscles. Immediately, he understood the importance of having strong arms. Basically, the arms can be divided into three groups: the biceps, the triceps, and the forearm/wrist. A variety of curls will thoroughly exercise the biceps while several different motions will exercise the triceps. For the forearm/wrist area, I recommend the "rice bucket," initially introduced by Steve Carlton and later made famous by Roger Clemens. Baseball TV analyst Tim McCarver, who actually caught for Carlton, once said, "Steve Carlton is the strongest man I've ever seen in baseball from the elbow to the fingertips." Carlton won four Cy Young Awards by throwing, among other pitches, a vicious curveball, the spin of which he generated by a violent snapping motion. Clemens, a six-time Cy Young winner, won with a 95 MPH fastball and biting slider early in his career and later with a virtually unhittable split-fingered fastball. With a combined ten Cy Young Awards between these two men, it might be in your best interest to emulate their forearm exercises.

Now, I could give you a "program" for you to use, but that's basically pointless. As I mentioned, weight training is so individualized that while one program may work fine for a certain player, another player may not find it beneficial at all. For the most part, though, exercising the same body part twice a week, with two or three days rest in between, is probably ideal for anyone under 21-years-old. Again, see what works for you. And remember that strength training, like hitting, pitching, and fielding, requires a consistent and lengthy program to obtain the results you seek. Rome wasn't built in a day.

Explosiveness training

When I was in spring training with the Houston Astros organization in 1998, GM Gerry Hunsicker spoke to us minor leaguers as a group about the effects of creatine, the muscle-building supplement. As an example, he used third baseman Ken Caminiti, not necessarily because he used creatine but because he had gained about 15 lbs. of muscle from the beginning of his career to that point. While it may have helped his power numbers as a hitter, Hunsicker equated the negative effects on his once-nonpareil defensive prowess to playing third base with a 15 lb.-weight draped over his shoulders. In other words, because Caminiti's body never became used to carrying the extra poundage, his defense suffered.

In the previous section of this chapter, I spoke about the importance of stretching to maintain the necessary fluidity for all baseball movements. Well, a similar effort must be made to counteract the newly added weight your body will now be carrying. To me, a quality program of "plyometrics" will fit the bill quite nicely.

Plyometrics is the general term for exercises designed to increase explosiveness, particularly within the legs. I mentioned the importance of footwork as an infielder, so certainly any additional quickness you can gain with your first step will help you immensely. Personally, I began doing plyometrics religiously as a senior in college. I don't know how much they helped my defense, but they definitely didn't hurt it.

I believe that the two best drills for increasing explosiveness and quickness are jumping rope and box jumps. Naturally, any athlete knows what jumping rope looks like. To some, it may seem like a horribly antiquated exercise, but if boxers, who are among the best athletes in the world in my opinion, still jump rope regularly, then there must be *some* good in it. Furthermore, it is good not only for quickness but also for cardiovascular development, too. If you don't believe me, go out and skip rope — no double-jumping either!—for 20 minutes or so, and let me know how you feel.

Box jumps, when done properly, can be extremely beneficial to an athlete's footwork. Box jumps, when done improperly, can cause tendonitis and general joint pain. Like weight lifting, the age and physical maturity level of a young athlete must be considered first when determining a good plyometrics program. Again, with a teenager, I believe it is better to err on the side of caution than on the side of overwork. The box jump drill is quite simple yet quite taxing. I recommend starting with a solid base (it doesn't have to be a box, *per se*) elevated between 18" and 24" above the floor, depending, of course, on the athlete's natural ability to leap. Now, have the athlete climb upon the box, dismount onto the floor, and then spring back up again. That is one repetition. The key part to the exercise is to bounce up *immediately* after contacting the floor. (For visual purposes, our college strength coach would tell us that we were landing on hot coals.) Once you've bounded back onto the box, gather yourself, and repeat. Remember, it is far better to pause at the top than on the floor. Also, this is *not* a "speed" drill. By that, I mean how many reps you can do in 30 seconds is irrelevant. This drill is designed to build explosiveness, so take your time and do it right.

I recommend doing four or five sets of 12 to 20 reps three times per week. Like weight training, "more" does not necessarily mean "better." Listen to your body, especially to your knees. It is far more beneficial to start with a simple, light workout and graduate to a more difficult one than it is to overdo it from Day One and put undue stress on your joints. Just as you can't expect to improve your hitting, pitching, or fielding overnight, don't expect to improve your explosiveness overnight. However, a plyometrics program performed properly and religiously over two or three months will noticeably increase your first-step quickness.

The Perception Factor

One thing I used to hate when I was an amateur was hearing about scouts' evaluations and the term "body type." My attitude was, "So what if I'm not chiseled out of marble? I can play." It's amazing how times have changed. As a college baseball coach, one of the things I look for in a young ballplayer is, in fact, his body type. We coaches and scouts will label a player as "good body" or a "bad body." Certainly, a good body is no guarantee of success when it comes to actually playing baseball just as a bad body is no forbearer of ineptitude. As evaluators, though, we have to consider a player not just for next year but for the next *four* years. Is this player going to gain a lot of weight in a college environment? Is this player, who is skinny and weak now, going to fill out someday?

As a teenage boy, dieting is probably the furthest thing from your mind. However, your diet will have a direct bearing on your perception. If you're skinny, eat. If you're on the thick side, watch what you eat. To be sure, skinny people who try to put on weight oftentimes have great difficulty in doing so, much to the chagrin of those trying to lose weight.

Yes, you are genetically bound to your body type, but do what you can to counteract it. For example, I played with a guy in Class A who ate Taco Bell every night for dinner (or so it seemed), and he never gained a pound. I, on the other hand, used to go to the grocery store and buy chicken and lean cuts of beef to prepare for dinner because the alternative — fast food every night — would undoubtedly put too much weight on me. Take control to the best of your ability.

In terms of length, this chapter appears to be the least important, and that is by design. Obviously, strength is very important to the success of a ballplayer, but excessive weightlifting at a young age, I feel, can impede his progress, not help it. I believe it is far more beneficial to a player's future to concentrate on honing his skills — especially while he is still growing — and leave the weight training until later. Remember, any fool can go into a gym or health club "get ripped"; only a few can combine a fluid swing and some muscle into one dangerous package. Hit the tee before you hit the weights.

8

Making the Grade

The importance of getting good grades

When I recruited the University of North Carolina during my senior year of high school (yes, you read that right; I feel that I "recruited" them since I initiated everything), head coach Mike Roberts had never seen me play. I sent him a videotape of my hitting and fielding, and, apparently, he had some "scouts" in the area who verified my ability to him. Of course, I included my stellar academic record with my correspondence. As I reflect now on my college recruiting process, I am simply amazed at how I ended up at UNC. In 1989, just two years earlier, UNC had been in the College World Series, and now, they were considering me for a scholarship? Sure, I had good stats as a high school ballplayer and was always a top player in my section, but then again, Western Pennsylvania isn't exactly a hotbed of baseball talent. Physically, the same shortcomings that haunted me as a pro—no footspeed, average arm strength, little power—were equally slight as a prep athlete. So, how in Sam Hill did I end up at UNC?

Well, look at some facts. (1) In 1991, UNC, as a part of the state university system, was required to take a minimum of 83 percent of its incoming class from within the state of North Carolina. Naturally, a small percentage of the out-of-state enrollees are athletes in the 26 intercollegiate sports UNC offers. As you may or may not know, every college coach is afforded a few "at-risk" athletes on his submission list. These athletes are average high school students at best, but since they are top-notch athletes and UNC has such a rich tradition of athletics, they are admitted nevertheless. Because a coach has only a small handful of young men for this list every year, he reserves them for the blue-chipper recruits. After all, brains and brawn rarely exist in the same package. Why would he waste a valuable spot on an average athlete? (2) At the end of 1990–91 academic year, the men's baseball program finished 26th out of the 26 intercollegiate athletic teams at UNC in terms of overall G.P.A. Evidently, unless Coach Roberts started to make some rapid improvements, his job might have been in jeopardy. He couldn't afford to bring in another at-risk freshman to lower his team's already paltry G.P.A. (3) In 1991, a college baseball program could offer no more scholarship money than the equivalent of 13 full, out-of-state athletic scholarships. This money could be divided in any way the head coach saw fit, and, as you would expect, the better the recruit, the more of that money he would receive.

I think Coach Roberts took a certain pride in having players from all over the country in his program. I can't blame him. If I were a major college coach, I would want the satisfaction of knowing that I could land the best talent in the country, regardless of from whence the talent came. Roberts also knew that my academics would not be a problem, as they are with many incoming freshmen. He probably also suspected that he could get me to go to UNC for next to nothing (he succeeded).

When I arrived at UNC, I was amazed at the talent there. Physically, I was outclassed. In retrospect I can honestly say that about the only thing I could do well was hit left-handed. I was a garbage right-handed hitter, I had an average arm for a major college third baseman, I had no idea how to field a groundball properly, and I couldn't run. In contrast, my roommate had just been drafted by Oakland that summer, mostly because he could run, hit, and throw very well for a high school player. Another incoming freshman could have played football at U. of Tennessee and had excellent power. The shortstop on the team was a sophomore, and after his senior year of high school, Detroit drafted him in the second round. It didn't take me long — or Coach Roberts, as it turned out — to see that I was overmatched. At the end of the year, he basically ran me out of the program, but I'll save that story for another day.

Were you able to piece all of this together? It appears that Coach Roberts used me. In fact, Mark Kingston, a senior on the team and a good friend of mine to this day, used to tease me that the only reason I was at UNC was to bring up the team G.P.A. Obviously, I was "over-recruited," by Coach Roberts, but perhaps there was a bit of truth to Mark's insinuation. Regardless, I can say that, for one year, I donned the Carolina Blue and was on scholarship at one of the premier academic-athletic institutions in the country. And don't think for a minute that Jay Phillips, who recruited me for Virginia Tech during the summer, didn't take that fact into consideration.

The importance of good grades, Part 2

This section may not have a lot to do with high school, but I want you to understand how important it is to take pride in your schoolwork. On May 17th, 1992, during my exit interview with Coach Roberts, he told me that he didn't think I was a Division I baseball player at the UNC level at that time. He told me that I could return for my sophomore year, but there was no guarantee that I would make the team. He added that if I chose to return and failed to make the team, I could still have my scholarship. At the time, I was devastated. What good was college to me if I couldn't play baseball? Roberts knew how important baseball was to me, and by the time he finished saying those words to me, he knew I was leaving. (Of the nine freshmen from my incoming class, I think only five went back for their sophomore year.)

During the first semester of my freshman year, I earned a 3.46 G.P.A., easily the highest on the team. Granted, I took only 13 units (I dropped a history class due its conflicting with our practice schedule), but it was a nice start to my college career. The combination of regular practice, Mark's and my intense pre- and post-practice hitting sessions, and hitting the books at night made for an exhausting semester, but it was worth it: I got the grades that I wanted, and I could feel myself getting better at baseball, too. I felt a tremendous sense of accomplishment over that Christmas break.

During the spring semester, my grades slipped somewhat, as do most college ballplayer's during baseball season. When you play 60 games as we did, you miss a lot of class. Yes, with study hall and the make-up opportunities that most professors offer, it is possible to get good marks in the spring, but there is just no substitute for being in class. I ended the spring with a 2.46 G.P.A. for 13 units, leaving me with a 2.96 G.P.A. for the year. It's a good thing my academic work didn't wane because when I decided to transfer, it turned out that I needed those good grades.

Virginia Tech is by no means a Harvard, but neither is it a community college. Every year, the admissions department, like at all universities, has to turn down a couple of potential recruits due to the university's academic standards. Furthermore, at the time of my recruitment, I was told that, in the past, the admissions department had frowned upon taking in transfer students. Normally, they said, incoming students aren't able to transfer their previous courses into Virginia Tech credits. Fortunately, though, UNC is a widely respected institution, so Virginia Tech accepted all 26 of my credits. My college baseball career — and college experience in general — was the best time of my life, and it afforded me the chance to play professional baseball. Had I drifted through my freshman year, as many freshmen do, I may not have been able to transfer to VT. I can say unequivocally that my decision to transfer to Virginia Tech is the single best decision of my life, and it was possible because I took pride in the "student" part of being a student-athlete. If you want to realize your dreams, *you can leave nothing to chance.* I didn't. Will you?

9

Being Seen

When I began writing this book, during the winter of 2001–02, I was still a player. I didn't officially retire until mid-March of 2002, and the vast majority of this work was completed by the time I became an assistant coach at UNC-Charlotte. During the final editing process, which occurred during the summer of 2002, I had already done quite a bit recruiting — scouting, if you will — of local and national high school players. While I already had a pretty decent idea of what colleges look for, my new career gave me an inside look into the minds of intercollegiate coaches. I am now able to share this information with you.

One of the most common questions I receive is, "I'm from Backwoods, USA. How can I be noticed?" You may be the best-looking girl in the bar, but if you hide in the corner all night long, very few people will see you. Certainly, having baseball people at least *know* of you is immensely important, and in order to get your name out there, you must do the self-marketing.

It's no secret that California, Florida, and Texas are traditional hotbeds of baseball talent. All you have to do is look at a major league roster, and you'll see what I mean. But why? Yes, the year-round, baseball-friendly climate allows the youths of these regions to play more baseball than the northern kids, but I don't think that is the reason. In fact, if you were to take a hypothetical cross-section of the athletic talent of, say, Hartford, Connecticut, and Dallas, Texas, I don't think you would see much of a difference. The two big advantages the Sun Belt kids have are exposure to baseball people and a chance to play baseball almost year-round. They are forever playing games, participating in tournaments and showcases, and attending camps in the hopes increasing their chances of being seen. So, how do you, who spends only four months per year on baseball fields, compete?

Well, there are a few answers. You can move to a Sun Belt locality, but that's usually not an option. You can forsake all other sports to focus on baseball, and, in doing so, spend your "offseasons" attending camps and tournaments. Or, you can do what I did: play four sports in high school and send out résumés and videotapes to colleges. There is no guarantee that my method will work for you (heck, it almost didn't work for *me*), but what other choices do you have?

For example, when I was a 16-year-old, I played Big League baseball. We didn't have American Legion baseball in Armstrong County, so all the 16- to 18-year-olds played this level of baseball. I was selected to our district's All-Star team, and we competed in a regional tournament in Delaware in the summer of 1989. We lost our only two games in the double-elimination tournament — pretty badly, might I add. Earlier that year, I had my breakout spring as a sophomore, hitting .469 and being named to the all-section team. I thought I was "being seen," but I had no idea that no one was seeing me. Whenever my mom or I would contact a college baseball program, the coach would always ask, "What Legion team does he play for?" After explaining to him that I didn't play American Legion baseball, he would say, "Big League? I never heard of that." It was pretty apparent where I needed to be.

The following summer, four pretty good players from my high school and I decided to travel to Freeport, about 20 minutes away, to play for its American Legion team. In doing so, we caused a minor controversy in Kittanning (Pennsylvania) because the local Big League team was losing some its best talent to the American Legion team in Freeport. Obviously, none of us cared. We all had college aspirations, and playing Big League baseball wasn't going help us achieve that end.

I seriously doubt that anyone saw me more easily because I was playing American Legion baseball — this was, of course, Western Pennsylvania — but I knew *no one* was going to see me in Big League. We were playing out in the middle of nowhere against, sometimes, guys who showed up for games in hip-waders ten minutes late. It was as far away from college baseball as you could possibly be, and I needed to make a change. Fortunately, the Freeport situation worked out well, and I was able to play two solid summers at the American Legion level before going off to college.

What I look for

First of all, when I say 'I', I am referring to college coaches everywhere because we all look for the same basic things in a high school player. Perhaps the tool I look for most often in a player is speed. There is an old saying in baseball that says, "Speed never slumps." If a coach decides you can't play the infield, he can move you to the outfield—but only if you can run. No, you don't have to be a jackrabbit to play right or left field, but it certainly helps. Also, speed causes headaches for the defense, especially at the college level, where defensive lapses are frequent. You don't even have to be a base-stealing threat. If you can run, ground balls in the infield can cause problems. You can go first-to-third more easily. You can go second-to-home more easily. In short, you have an extra dimension in your game.

But speed is relative to the position you play. Traditionally, coaches like their "speed" guys to be up the middle, *i.e.*, second basemen, shortstops, and centerfielders because speed is more important at these positions than at the others on the field. Now, don't confuse running speed with foot quickness, as the former doesn't always guarantee the latter. Middle infielders need foot quickness, not speed, but, usually, if a player has a running speed, he has foot quickness, too. It's not always the case, but most of the time it is.

So, what if you're a middle infielder who doesn't run well (when I say "well," I mean a 6.8 seconds or better 60-yard-dash)? Again, let me speak from experience. I was a shortstop in high school, not because I possessed shortstop-caliber skills but because I was the best athlete on the team. Anyone who recruited me would have projected me as a corner infielder because of my body type and lack of footspeed (I think my best 60-yard-dash time as a high school student was 7.25). Unfortunately, I think one of the reasons I was lightly recruited in high school was because I was a third baseman playing shortstop. When I went to tryouts—either for a professional team or for the American Legion showcase game—I was listed as a shortstop because that was the position I played for my high school and American Legion teams. I didn't occur to me at the time that I was being graded as a shortstop, a position for which I was ill-suited. I should have been listed as a third baseman but because I had no idea what the hell I was doing, I was killing myself.

Also, I look for athleticism. This term is certainly vague, but you know what I mean. I look for someone who moves like an athlete, someone who is light on his feet and has a sense of body control. However, don't confuse bat speed, foot speed, or arm strength with athleticism. As I mentioned, Michael Jordan is one of the greatest athletes ever, and his bat speed and arm strength were probably average at best. Remember, as a college coach, I am thinking about a three- or four-year plan for a high school student. Most college coaches believe that a young, athletic, raw high school baseball player who can hit very well against high school pitching can be molded into a polished, "draftable" collegiate junior or senior. We believe that we can teach him how to play a position best suited to his ability level. We can teach him how to run the bases properly. We can teach him a solid mental approach to hitting. But it's difficult to teach these skills to someone without the natural athleticism to incorporate them.

The showcases

If you possess the aforementioned traits and you aren't playing in Antarctica, in this day and age of Internet and cell phones, someone will find you. The days of going to the backwoods of Oklahoma and finding the next Mickey Mantle are virtually over. But what if you're a marginal player who has the desire but lacks the eye-popping tools to compete and improve at the college level? Well, fortunately, one of the upsides to the "Internetization" of amateur baseball is that in just about every part of the country, there is some website/service geared towards getting players to college baseball. For example, TeamOneBaseball.com is a very popular recruiting service among high school athletes and college and pro scouts. PerfectGame.org is another that has arisen recently. Each organization is great for the players because they get to work out in front of scouts and evaluators, and the scouts and evaluators get a chance to see the area's best players in one fell swoop.

But buyer beware. A lot of these services may make allegations and promises of college scholarships to athletes who have no chance of playing at the Division I level. In short, a lot of them are moneymakers. Sure, the majority of the athletes who attend these workouts may indeed be of Division I caliber, but several may not. Most of them require a substantial fee to participate in one of their "showcases," which leads to me to believe that the people in charge of these services are not hurting for cash. Unfortunately, if you are one of the "unseen," you really don't have another choice. If the college coaches and scouts haven't seen you play enough, then the recruiting services are often your last resort.

The only way to find out which services are reputable and which aren't is to do your homework. It may mean talking to a former pupil of the service. It may mean contacting a collegiate coach for advice. It may mean doing the research yourself to see how many of the students have gone on to the Division I level. A lot of them may promise gold at the end of the rainbow, so be careful. Also, in fairness to the services, you must be objective about your own ability. After all, it wouldn't make much sense for the service to turn away a cash-paying client just because he is a lousy baseball player. People today don't want to admit that they are deficient at something, especially at something they love, and they certainly don't want to hear the bad news from somebody else. If you have an inflated opinion about your own ability, you may be pouring your money down the drain because no college coach or scout is going to consider you if you stink.

Grades

Believe it or not, grades can play an important part in a college coach's perception of you. There are some private schools that are among the elite programs in the country, and they just don't accept any high school superstar off the street. Some of them have extremely high academic requirements, such as a 3.5 G.P.A. and an 1100 SAT score. Yes, sometimes they can sneak a player or two in despite an inferior academic record, but it is rare. If you look at the some of the top private universities in the college baseball world they rarely have junior college players on their squads because of their admissions standards. (Usually, the reason a Top 20 program-caliber player goes to a junior college in the first place is because he had lousy grades and/or SAT scores as a prep athlete.)

I've been at showcases where a coach may really be interested in a player only to turn to his personal information and find out that he would be inadmissible to a poor academic standing. The coach has no choice but to turn his interests elsewhere. Suppose you have dreams of playing for the previous year's national champion. Suppose you were capable of doing better academically than what you're grades have shown. How would you feel if that school's recruiter had seen you play but decided not to pursue you due to your shoddy classroom performance? Every single thing counts.

Play, play, play

One final comment about being seen. In the summer of 1991, the summer before I went to college, I was playing for both the American

Legion team and a local men's league team. I think I was playing five or six games a week. I cannot emphasize enough how important it is to *play*, not only to be seen but also to improve. You never know who is watching, and all it takes sometimes is being on the right field in front of the right college coach and playing a great game for your baseball career to take off. Moreover, you may find yourself playing with or against someone who knows someone in the baseball world (with my new coaching position, I am amazed at how small the baseball world is). If you make a good impression on him, he may refer to someone else. You just never know.

Furthermore, I can remember feeling myself becoming better and better by July, and, as a shortstop, I was making some plays that I could not have made in March. I was *playing* and therefore improving. Unless you have something else more important to do, play, play, play!

10

Selecting the Right College

Trying to decide where to attend college is usually the first major, life-altering decision a young person makes in his or her life, and a great deal of the rest of his or life is a reflection of that choice. As a baseball player, the decision is even more difficult because you have to determine if the institution in question can satisfy you not only intellectually and socially but also athletically. Like selecting a spouse or a job or a vehicle, choosing a college or university that best suits your needs is a difficult and an extremely important decision. It requires a lot of time and energy should definitely not be taken lightly.

First things first

I was lightly recruited out of high school. When I say lightly recruited, I mean my parents had to pay for all but one of the thirteen schools I visited during my senior year. Basically, I did the recruiting. Part of the problem was that I was not from a traditional hotbed of baseball talent, but part of it was due to my parents' and my ignorance of the whole recruiting process. I was a good student and a good ballplayer, but beyond that, we knew nothing. Chances are, if you're reading this, you are entering into the same abyss as I was over a decade ago. I want to use this chapter to share with you, as a potential collegiate student-athlete, some of my personal experiences to help you make arguably the most important decision of your life.

When I was a kid growing up in Western Pennsylvania, I was a pretty fair athlete at whatever sport I played, from my earliest Little League days to my final year of high school. Starting in the spring of my sophomore year of high school, when I burst onto the scene as a baseball player, it seemed that my picture was in a local newspaper every other week or so. A lot of it had to with the fact that I was a top-notch student who was playing four sports, but most of it was due to my exploits on the fields, courts, or rinks. My parents, however, had enough vision to understand that being "the man" in Kittanning (pop. 10,000), Pennsylvania, does not guarantee success beyond the high school ranks, and they did a good job, for a while, of trying to keep me humble and grounded. My father satisfied his athletic id as a collegiate athlete, and, thus, he understood how small time high school sports are in the big picture; in other words, he didn't suffer from "Al Bundy Syndrome," an affliction that causes a slightly overweight, usually balding, somewhat intoxicated man to recount his vastly exaggerated high school exploits to men of a similar ilk.

The problem, though, is that when you're always in the newspapers, you start to believe you're entitled to red-carpet treatment. It wasn't as though I went around telling everyone that I was Superman; it was that inside me, I felt that college recruiters should be lining up at my door, *begging* me to come play for their schools. After all, I was a star student-athlete, and I could play for any college baseball team in the country. How wrong I was. Not only did the colleges not line up, I had to recruit *them*. Or, more accurately, my mother had to recruit them. If it weren't for her tireless efforts, I probably wouldn't be typing this right now.

Controlling what you can control (heard this before?)

To me, the first part of finding your ideal college or university is to control everything you can control. Let me explain. In pro baseball, there are so many factors that you can't control working against you — age, a worldwide talent pool, foot speed, bat speed, arm strength, etc.— that you *must* control those things that you can — attitude, hustle, work ethic, and keeping your nose clean. The same holds true for the college recruiting process, except those controllable things are, among other things, your grades and your attitude in school. Look, as much as you'd like to think so (as I did at that age), you can't control your talent level, namely those things I mentioned above. There will always—*always*— be someone out there with more ability than you, so you can't expect your own athletic talents to be the sole reason for a college coach to come see you.

Looking back, no one ever had to tell me to get good grades. Part of my intensely competitive nature was to be better than everyone at everything, including schoolwork. I wanted to be better at sports than the jocks and better at school than the nerds. Because I respected — and feared — my dad, following rules and respecting authority was not a problem either. No teacher or principal or counselor could ever label me a "bad kid."

Matters of *el corazon* are a little tougher to control, but you need to make wise decisions in that area of your life as well. If you *must* engage in sexual relations, do so responsibly; trying to raise a child and make it to the big leagues is about as easy as climbing Mt. Everest without oxygen or clothing. I'm not going to tell you how to run your love life, but let me say this: there are several thousand fish in the sea in college. Do not let one in high school negatively affect your life to the point that you cannot perform at your best. Also, if you're hanging out with a bad crowd, I suggest that you break away from it. Remember the Allen Iverson bowling alley incident in 1993? Here was an innocent kid in the wrong place at the wrong time, but since he was Mr. Superstar Athlete, he took the fall. Where there's smoke, there's fire. Again, though, you must have the maturity and foresight to be able to make such profound decisions.

Now that you've kept your nose clean, gotten good grades, and put up good numbers on the baseball field, you're ready to proceed. Now, I'm not going to be one of those people who will tell you that your first priority is to get an education; that's entirely up to you and your own motivation. One bit of advice I received in high school is to choose a college at which you'd be happy to be a student if you were suddenly unable to play baseball. Baloney. Yes, injuries happen, but baseball injuries are rarely career-ending, especially for a college-aged kid.

Do your homework

Look, sitting on your ass and waiting for the colleges to fall into your lap is faulty logic at best. No doubt, if you're a blue-chip talent, word will get around, but I'm guessing that your reading this means that you're not. *You* have to get on the phone and the Internet. *You* have to go to college baseball camps. *You* have to put together the videotape and resume. Of course, you don't *have* to, but again, it all comes down to how badly you want to play college baseball. Let me give you an example.

I became friends with a guy in California who was a pretty good prep baseball player. He didn't have great "tools," but he was a damn good hitter. Well, he enrolled at a junior college (juco) in California, and if you don't know anything about how they work, let me explain. Each fall, the head baseball coach brings in scores of players because a lot of players may decide at the last moment not attend the juco, so the more players a coach can get to enroll, the better. While this situation may not exactly be fair to the players trying to make the team, the coach benefits from the huge talent pool from which he can build his team. Anyway, my friend got to this juco, only to find that his professors were lousy, his living situation was terrible, and that something like 90 players were trying to make the team. In a matter of a few weeks, he left the juco. That tells me two things: (1) he didn't do his homework and (2) he wasn't very serious about playing college baseball. This same friend tried to walk on at a local four-year college, but he failed to make the team. I wanted to tell him, "Look, if your only chance of playing college baseball means traveling to Aberdeen, SD, to play at the Division III level, then you get your ass to South Dakota. Otherwise, don't bitch and moan to me about 'getting screwed' or 'not catching a break' or 'being treated unfairly'." If you think life ain't fair, try baseball.

The hard part of the entire process is determining what school best fits your ability level, so you have to be objective about your own ability and persistent enough to do your homework about the schools you have in mind. If you are lucky enough to have a school pay for you to visit it, then be as dogged in your questioning as you can. Ask everyone from the starting shortstop to the walk-on middle reliever what he thinks about the coach and the program. When I went to visit UNC during my senior year of high school, shortstop Keith Grunewald, a second round draft pick the previous spring, showed me around the campus and talked to me about the program. Naturally, as a supremely talented ballplayer whom every coach in the country would have loved to have on his team, Keith didn't see the less than positive things going on within the program. Or, perhaps, he saw them but just didn't care. After all, he was pretty much guaranteed the starting shortstop position as long as he was in Chapel Hill. Therefore, he never told me about the litany of complaints that other players had. I never spoke with the outgoing seniors, guys who had at one time lived and died for baseball but now were just going through the motions. You *must* do your homework to avoid being trapped in a tough situation.

It's funny because during my junior year at Virginia Tech, a freshman (who will remain anonymous) joined the team. We were eerily similar people: Pennsylvanians, good students, hard workers, infielders, switch-hitters. One day, we were talking about the whole college recruiting process, and I told him that I had spent my freshman year at UNC. He told me that UNC had shown some mild interest in him but that he never really gave the Tar Heels much consideration. By asking around, he had learned some of the negatives of the program that I had only realized through joining it. He had made what proved to be the right decision for him; I had not.

Playing up vs. playing down

One option is to attend one of the "baseball factories," schools that bring in recruits by the handful for a weeding out process. If you're good enough to be recruited by one of these schools, there's nothing wrong with biting off more than you can chew, but proceed with caution. Oftentimes, guys who could start at other schools end up sitting the bench at these places. The best way to determine what your playing time situation will be is to see what kind of scholarship money the coach has given you. No coach is going to give a huge chunk of his paltry scholarship allotment to a guy who is going to ride the pine. College coaches, rightly or wrongly, are judged on their win/loss records, so he will play the best players available to him. But, he will also think to himself, "Jeez, I gave this kid a lot of money; I better give him every opportunity to prove himself before I sit him — and his scholarship money — on the bench."

If you do decide to take your chances with the big scholarship money at a factory and things don't work out, transfer as soon as possible. There is nothing wrong with rolling the dice with a baseball powerhouse, but if you feel you will eventually be lost in the shuffle, get the hell out of there while you still have a collegiate career in front of you. That's exactly what the graduating seniors told me at the end of my freshman year. They knew how hungry I was to improve, so they advised me to move on. Thankfully, I did, and everything else worked out fine.

Another downside of the factories is that most of them overrecruit. That means they will often bring in 25 or so new players in the fall for the big "weed out": they keep the ones they want and discard the others. In this day and age, when college baseball has become almost as competitive as college football and basketball, it's not a secret that the big schools operate in this way. They simply bank on the fact that enough blue-chip recruits will say, "I know what the odds are, but they certainly would never cut *me*." The factories recruit from a quantity standpoint, and as long as this method continues to produce Omaha-bound teams, they will continue to do so.

The other option is to choose a school that is beneath your ability level, even though you probably won't improve as much as you would playing against better competition. The key to improving as a baseball player is to play as many *games* as possible; all the practice and drills and weightlifting in the world will only get you so far. While you may be the big fish in the small pond, at least you will be playing every day. If that's the case and you're not being challenged in the college season, do what you can to play in a quality summer league, especially one of the Major League Baseball-endorsed wooden bat leagues. Scouts who may have missed you during the spring may then get to see you in the summer.

If I had to choose one way or the other, I would opt for playing down a level as opposed to up a level. I cannot stress enough how important it is to *play* as many games per year as you can. It is extremely difficult to improve your skills by practice alone, not to mention the mental anguish that comes with sitting on the bench. While saying that you play baseball at a baseball power university may be quite an ego trip, are you actually *playing*? Or are you pulling splinters from your backside? Yes, facing top-notch collegiate pitching or hitting will undoubtedly make you a better hitter or pitcher, but you actually have to be out there on the field.

Finally, when it comes to professional scouts, there is a saying: If you're good enough, they'll find you. As I mentioned, with the Internet and the globalization of baseball, rarely anymore does a player slip through the cracks in the system. In other words, if you're even marginal pro ball material, at least one scout will see you play, no matter where you're in college. What that scout thinks about you is a different matter altogether, but at least you'll have had a chance to show your skills. Work hard, improve, keep your nose clean, and you'll get your shot.

11

The College Experience

My parents are both Cornell University graduates. My dad was there from the fall of 1963 to the spring of 1970, and my mom was enrolled from the fall of 1966 to the spring of 1970. While they didn't exactly indulge in the extracurricular activities that most college students of the tumultuous late 1960s did — I will *never* forgive them for not taking part in Woodstock, which took place only a few miles from them in the summer of 1969 — they nevertheless enjoyed their time in Ithaca, NY. As far back as I can remember, they always preached to my brother, my sister, and me that college is "the best four years of your life." They spoke of the parties and the freedom and meeting of new people, and, to me, it seemed like paradise. In fact, I can recall, at the ripe old age of ten, having to leave prematurely an afternoon of street hockey with some friends in order to go home and tend to the farm animals. As I stomped away from my friends in disgust, I thought to myself, "I can't wait to get to college, where no one can make me do anything I don't want to do." As it turned out, I loved my college experience as much as my parents did, if not more.

At Cornell in the 1960s, the students' motto was "Freedom with responsibility," which basically means you can do whatever you want provided you are accountable for your actions. While other colleges may not use those words verbatim, they are implied. For the first time in your life, you will be without parental supervision, and what can be better than that? No one to tell you to clean up your room. No one to tell you to study. No one to tell you to go pick up your brother from basketball practice. Heck, at a lot of colleges, even attending class is optional. Ah, but there is a catch: you now must answer not to your parents but to yourself. Can you handle this newfound liberation? Or will you, like Pinocchio, find yourself turning into a donkey in the face of such autonomy?

144

Why are you here?

No, this is not an existentialist-type question. I am not asking you to determine your place in the universe; I just want you to figure out what you hope to accomplish in your college experience. Are you in college to meet your future bride? Are you looking to go to medical school? Do you want to play in the big leagues? Obviously, I cannot answer this question. You must. And once you decide what you want out of college, you must make each decision according to reaching that goal.

When I arrived in Chapel Hill in August of 1991, I had no idea what my major would be. Oh, sure, stuff like orthopedic surgery was interesting to me, as was sports medicine, but I wasn't ready to make that kind of commitment. Nor was I interested in meeting the future Mrs. Durkac. All I cared about was playing baseball. To me, college without baseball was not an option, and my goal was not Duke Medical School or Wharton Business School; it was major league baseball. Naturally, I was going to take my education seriously, but from Day One, the academic part of college was never in my heart the way that baseball was.

In high school, which was relatively easy for me, I did the extra work required maintain a high grade point average. Throughout my high school years, being a top-notch student was as important to me as being a top-notch athlete. In college, however, that burning desire to succeed academically was overridden by desire to succeed athletically. Therefore, instead of doing extra bookwork in my free time, I spent it lifting weights or practicing my hitting. Even when I wasn't honing my baseball skills, I was reading about baseball or watching baseball videos. To put it bluntly, baseball became an obsession, the same way an overzealous man or woman stalks the object of his or her desire, and everything else in my life became unimportant.

The social scene

If you've ever seen a movie about college life —*Animal House, Revenge of the Nerds, Higher Learning,* etc.— you pretty much know what kind of temptations exist in the social scene. If college is about anything, it's about personal freedom, and, more specifically, the freedom to do just about whatever you want. If you have a vice, there's an exceptional chance that on any given campus across America, someone or something can meet your need. Like drugs? Marijuana, speed, Ecstasy, acid, and other mind-altering substances are easily obtainable. Like alcohol?

Parties run wild all weekend long at fraternity and sorority houses, apartment complexes, and dormitories. Like to gamble? I can virtually guarantee you that every major college in America has had some kind of illegal betting occurring on its campus at some point. Like girls? Well, let's just say that college girls experience the same freedom that college men do. Once again, you must ask yourself, "Why am I here?"

A wise man once suggested that the key to life is moderation, and if you carry that same attitude in college, you really can't go wrong. There is nothing wrong, in my opinion, with hitting the party scene on the weekends, or, once you are of legal age, hitting the bars and clubs once or twice a week. If you didn't *ever* participate in these rites of passage, I would think that you're missing out on some valuable social development. But do you have the maturity to prevent the late hours from disrupting your athletic and academic endeavors? Believe me, it's easy to ditch class after a rough night of partying. After you do it once, like any "crime," it becomes easier to do. After a semester of this type of frivolous behavior, you may find yourself staring at academic ineligibility, which would keep you from what I thought was the one true love of your life. If you let things you can control, *i.e.*, the decisions you make, negatively affect your baseball career, I have no sympathy for you.

If I may, let me give you personal story about choices. I enjoyed the nightlife of college as much as anyone. I spent more than a fair share of my time in the bars of Chapel Hill, North Carolina, and Blacksburg, Virginia. I entered my senior year of college in the fall of 1994 probably 15 pounds heavier than what I needed to be, and certainly, the barley and hops I was consuming frequently wasn't making weight loss any easier. I knew that in order to make myself more appealing to scouts in the following spring, I would have to shed the excess poundage. By Christmas break, though, I hadn't really done a whole lot about it.

During the holidays, I had a conversation with my friend Mark, who had finished his third year of pro ball. He knew how badly I wanted to play in the pros, and he was flabbergasted that I hadn't made a concerted effort to lose weight. He said to me, point-blank, "I can't believe you would let something you can control keep you from your dreams" (gee, where have you heard *that* before?). That conversation was all the impetus I needed, and from that day on, I didn't touch a drop of alcohol until March. It may not seem like a big deal, but it wasn't easy for me. I would go out as always with the guys, who thought I would cave in within two weeks, and drink Diet Coke instead of alcohol. I didn't cave in, however, because I had pro aspirations. As it turned out, I played my entire senior season at 205 pounds, my ideal playing weight. While I wasn't officially drafted, at least I did everything I could to make myself as marketable as possible.

Baseball

In the early 1990s, the NCAA incorporated a new series of rules that severely handcuffed the amount of time coaches have with their players, and these rules are still in place. When I was in college, a lot of coaches talked about the good ol' days playing three-hour intrasquad scrimmages every day in the fall — after a two-hour practice. Those days, I'm sad to say, are long gone. Now, any games played in the fall must be counted against total number of games a program is allotted (56) in the spring. Because coaches are afforded a minimal number of hours per week of practices and games, it is up to a player to work on his own, or with other players, to improve himself.

When I was at Virginia Tech, where winters can be — and were, when I was there — rather harsh, we had to practice indoors in the Rector Fieldhouse. That in itself wouldn't have been so bad except that we had to share it with other spring sports teams. Therefore, our practices were officially scheduled from 2:15 P.M. to 4:00 P.M. In these 105 minutes we had to warm-up, institute the various team plays (bunt coverages, 1st and 3rd steal defenses, infield-outfield communication, etc.) take a few swings, field a few groundballs, and condition. It was painfully obvious to me that I wasn't going to improve my individual skills in 30 minutes a day. In fact, one day, my persistent nagging for a coach to hit me more and more groundballs led the coach to ask me, "Jeez, Bo, how many are you going to take?" I said, much to the amusement of some eavesdropping teammates, "Don't worry, I'll let you know. Besides, you can't get to the Promised Land in two hours a day." I usually arrived at the fieldhouse at about 1:00 P.M. and stayed until 5:30. I knew I needed every extra minute to improve, and I used them.

To have a schedule like this, however, I needed to arrange my classes carefully, and, for about the 183rd time in this book, it's all about controlling what you can control and prioritizing. In the spring semesters I knew I needed to be done with class by 12:00 P.M. in order to eat lunch and make it to the fieldhouse by 1:00 P.M. As a springtime athlete, I was given priority over regular students at class selection time, and I never understood how some ballplayers were forced to miss part or all of a practice because of scheduling conflicts. Certainly, if you are in a major that offers a required course only at 3:00 P.M. on Wednesdays in the spring semester, then you are in trouble, but these are extenuating circumstances. A lot of times players would schedule their classes a little bit later in the morning to get an extra hour or two of sleep. Doing so meant that attending the last class of the day would prevent the student-athlete from arriving early to practice and thus prevent him using that valuable time to make himself better.

For my three springs at Virginia Tech, I had identical spring schedules: Monday-Wednesday-Friday classes from 9:00 A.M. to 11:50 A.M. and Tuesday-Thursday class from 9:30 A.M. to 10:45 A.M. (I took only the minimum number of required courses [4] in the spring due to the hectic travel schedule). With this schedule I was able to spend as much time as possible in the Fieldhouse. Other players may have used the free time in their equally light schedules to sleep or to hang out, but I had an agenda, and I had dreams.

Academics

Now, I am mentioning the academic part last for a reason, and I'll tell you why. I have always been one to question things that don't seem right to me. Along these lines, it seems so hypocritical to me that college coaches spend the majority of their recruitment talks to prospective students and their parents on academics, but my whole attitude towards the "student" part of student-athletes can be summed up in the following quotation. Don Nehlen, former longtime head football coach at West Virginia U., in the wake of the aforementioned new legislation by the NCAA, said, "I don't know what all these news rules are for. College today is no different from when I was in school: those who wanted to graduate, graduated, and those who wanted to monkey around, monkeyed around." I couldn't agree more. The academic part of college is no different from the athletic part of it, *i.e.*, you only get out what you put in. If you want to jerk around, get lousy grades, and perhaps lose your eligibility, then do that, but you'll have no one to blame but yourself.

Virginia Tech prides itself on having ample academic counselors for its athletes, going as far as making study hall mandatory for all incoming freshman, transfers, and those student-athletes whose GPA's were under a certain level. Looking back, our study hall at Virginia Tech, at least when I was there, was probably a microcosm of student-athletes across the nation: three-quarters of them were in there sleeping or talking or goofing off, and the other quarter were actually doing work. Just like high school, I feel that you shouldn't have to be motivated to do your work. Unfortunately, it has been my experience that the vast majority of college athletes do need some source of motivation.

What I am saying is that *you* have the final say in what happens academically in your college experience. I was amazed at how much free time I had during my freshman year of college. In high school, as a three- and four-sport athlete, my days usually began at 6:30 A.M. and ended at 10:00 P.M. In college, though, they began at 7:00 A.M. for classes and ended after our practice at about 5:30 P.M. As my college career progressed, the hours didn't change very much. After dinner, I had several hours to do whatever I wanted, and since I wanted to get decent grades, I studied. No, I didn't study as much as I should have, but I was never in danger of losing my eligibility. The same can't be said for a lot of my fellow ballplayers. Oh, well. Their loss, right? I believe that you can go to just about any accredited college or university in the country, and, if your grades are good enough, you'll be able to land a decent job. Certainly, a degree in finance from Stanford University or in pre-med from Princeton University will garner more attention than other degrees, but across the board, an undergraduate degree is an undergraduate degree, and at least you'll have a diploma. Then, if you are fortunate enough to play minor league ball for a few years, you'll be able to further your education once you decide you're ready.

Finally, I have a acquaintance who teaches at a major college baseball powerhouse, and she had a student say to her, in their first meeting, "I'm on the baseball team here, and since I'll be going pro someday, I don't care about my grades, and I'm not even going to study," or something along these lines. Just as this player, who is probably quite talented if he is playing baseball at this institution, would look at me on the baseball field and ask, "Damn, Bo, why can't you run and throw any better than that?" I would look at him in the classroom and ask him, "Damn, So-and-so, why do you have such a lousy attitude?" I guess I don't understand apathy over important, life-altering matters. What if this kid ends up academically ineligible for a spring semester? The coach may be so fed up with him that he might run him out of the program. Then, after he transfers, the kid may find himself in a less than desirable program, which would severely hinder his chances of going pro. Look, you don't have to be a brain surgeon to receive a four-year degree. If you just go to class every day and do the minimum amount of work required, you'll graduate easily. Apparently, some people just don't understand.

12

Dealing with Coaches

There's a saying that goes, "One should learn to enjoy the rain. Any fool can be happy when the sun shines." Think of this axiom and relate it to the coaching world. A good coach — someone who knows the game, who understands the psychology of an athlete, and who doesn't let his ego get in the way — is easy to play for. That's obvious. I have some bad news for you, though: there are a lot of bad coaches out there.

Now, when I say bad, there are three types of bad: (1) the coach who doesn't know anything about baseball, (2) the coach who doesn't know anything about psychology, and (3) the coach who doesn't understand — or doesn't remember — how difficult it is to hit or pitch a baseball and therefore can't relate to players who struggle. I promised a long time ago that I will *never* become one the coaches of the last category. The bottom line is that baseball a very, very difficult sport to learn.

Need evidence? Well, why is it that probably 90 percent of the athletes who go to college to play both football and baseball eventually gravitate towards football? The answer is simple: you can become an outstanding football player with sheer athleticism. With baseball, you need skills, and sheer athleticism does not always translate into these skills. Look at Michael Jordan, one of the greatest athletes of all time, and his struggles in baseball. To be sure, he hadn't played in fifteen years when he attempted to play Class AA for the Chicago White Sox, but he was nevertheless lousy at best. Even with a couple of years of seasoning, anyone who knew anything about baseball could see that he would never amount to a hitter. Andy Van Slyke said, "There will be peace in the Middle East before Michael Jordan ever gets a legitimate at-bat in the big-leagues."

To offer further credence about this lack of understanding, go to a college baseball game sometime, and watch the third base coach (often the head coach as well) over the course of the game. Count the number of times he either verbally or, even worse, nonverbally berates a hitter after the hitter takes a bad swing at a pitch or a pitcher when the pitcher walks a batter. To me, that is absolutely *not* the way to deal with failures, yet amateur coaches do it all the time. Now, I am not purporting that I have all the answers to coaching, but I do know one thing: baseball is a sport that definitely *not* ruled by emotion.

In basketball and football, a coach can give a rousing half-time speech and break a few chalkboards, and his team will come out ready to run through a brick wall. That emotion may carry the team to victory. Unfortunately, it just doesn't work that way in baseball. A coach can't scream at a player to get him to perform better. If that technique worked, then professional managers would do it to their players, and that rarely happens.

Even in the "emotion" sports, there are intellectual styles of coaching. Phil Jackson, of the Bulls and Lakers dynasties, comes to mind. Whether all of his Zen Buddhism and Native American references are the source of his coaching success remains to be seen, but he certainly doesn't appear to be a coach with the old school mentality. In football, Bill Walsh is considered to be a genius, and the fact that roughly two-thirds of all NFL teams run a version of his West Coast offense is reason enough. There is one story about Walsh during his days as Stanford University's head coach in the 1990s that I really like. Apparently, during a preseason drill, one of Walsh's assistant coaches was screaming like a maniac at one of his players for failing to execute the drill properly. Walsh in turn yelled at his coach, "Stop yelling and start teaching!"

And then, of course, there is my all-time favorite coach, former UCLA basketball coach John Wooden. Of all the things he did that separated himself from all the other coaches in the world, my personal favorite was how he almost *never* raised his voice during games. His attitude was, "If I haven't prepared my team — both mentally and physically — to play well today, then I have failed as a coach."

Finally, I have found, through my vast playing experiences, that rarely can you "will" a team to victory. In other words, you can't expect to have so-so practices and then be at your peak — as an individual or as a team — at game time. To sum up that thought, Bobby Knight said, "The will to win is not what's important. Everyone has that. It's the will to prepare to win that counts." It's true, isn't it? When the bell sounds at game time, everybody wants to win, but how badly do you want to prepare? Do you want to shoot those extra 100 jump shots? Do you want to run those 10 extra windsprints? Do you want to take those 30 extra groundballs?

Some bad examples

Did you ever notice how stoic New York Yankees manager Joe Torre is during games? He understands that once he puts his lineup card on the wall, he job is basically done for the day — with the exception, of course, of in-game substitutions. He knows that if his guys aren't mentally and physically prepared to play by the first pitch, then he either (1) has not done his job as a manager or (2) doesn't have on his team the right men for the job. If a guy makes a mental or physical error, does Torre berate him? Not in a million years. Maybe after the game he will discuss the gaffe with the player in a professional manner but never during the game. Why add insult to injury by chewing him out? If major league baseball managers understand that line of thinking, why don't college coaches

Let me give a few examples of what I'm talking about. I played with a guy who was a pitcher at a Big XII school in the mid–1990s, and the pitcher was shuffling between bullpen and starting duties. During a tournament early in his junior year (his first year at the school after two years of junior college), the head coach wasn't sure whom to start in a particular game against a top-notch opponent. The pitching coach recommended my former teammate, and the head coach agreed to start him. Well, due to excessive nerves, the pitcher struggled with his control in the first inning and gave up a couple of runs. The pitching coach went out to the mound for a discussion. According to the pitcher, the pitching coach said, his voice on the edge of shouting, "I stick my neck out for you to get you this start, and this is how you repay me?" Are you kidding me? If there was ever a "Baseball Psychology 101" course, this guy never took it. Maybe this motivational ploy would work on an outside linebacker, but not on a pitcher. And it didn't work, either; my former teammate lasted only two more innings and took the loss.

Another example. I was on a summer league team during my college days, and one day we were facing a pretty good pitcher (he went on to be a fourth-round draft pick). When a bunch of wooden bat-swinging college kids, who had spent the entire spring playing with aluminum bats, face a pitcher with a nice fastball, there are going to be a lot of late swings. When a hitter is late on a fastball, more often than not, he will hit the ball in the air. Well, after about three innings of watching us hit weak fly balls, our coach gave us an ultimatum: "The next time someone hits a fly ball, he's coming out of the game." Sure enough, he yanked our shortstop the next inning for just that. Once again, are you kidding me? This coach was an average player at best at a small Division II college in New York, and he obviously knew nothing — or remembered nothing — about the difficulty of hitting good pitching.

One coach I encountered is perhaps the best illustration of my point. To give you a peek inside his head, you needn't look any further than his ways of teaching hitting and fielding. Other players who had been on the team for some time told me that the style of hitting this coach was teaching that year was their fourth in four years. They said it was as if he had picked up a book on hitting during each offseason, seen a new theory on hitting, and then decided to introduce it to his team. The most bogus part of it all was that all of his teaching had to do with the stance, and if there's one thing I have come to loathe, it's a hitting instructor who teaches a certain stance. The results showed in his teams' consistently poor offensive statistics. Some of the players intimated that he took a certain pride in winning despite an anemic offense.

Defensively, what this coach taught is even more bizarre. As individualized as hitting is (just watch a big league game and you'll see the myriad different stances and swings of the hitters), there is basically only one correct to field a groundball (see the fielding chapter above). The sad part is that this coach even taught the wrong way to do *that*. I firmly believe that it is better to say nothing at all to a player than to offer him improper instruction, something that anyone who has played professionally can understand. Anyone who has played professionally has seen (1) the right way to do things and (2) that the players who are successful don't always look the same in doing so. It's a simple case of fundamentals versus styles, a section within the hitting chapter.

The "justification of paycheck" coaches

Unfortunately, though, a lot of amateur coaches at every level don't understand this point. They may think they can reinvent the game, but, deep down, they know they can't, and this sad but true fact brings me to the last type of bad coach: the "justification of paycheck" coach. One of the most difficult things for a coach to do is to recognize talent and leave it alone. Doing so requires a certain amount of pride swallowing, which is generally not an easy task for a coach. For example, take the manager of the 1986 Memphis Chicks (I can't recall his name) when he was told that Heisman trophy winner Bo Jackson was joining his club in the middle of the season. He said, "I have been given strict instructions on what to do with Bo. If I mess with him, they'll throw me into a river." Someone in the Kansas City Royals' front office was wise enough to recognize that Bo Jackson was one of the greatest physical specimens in sports history, perhaps the ultimate combination of speed and strength in one package — *ever* — and that "coaching" him would only foul him up.

As another example, take the "Fab Five" of University of Michigan basketball in the early 1990s. When Chris Webber, Jalen Rose, Juwon Howard, Ray Jackson, and Jimmy King arrived in Ann Arbor in the fall of 1991, they represented the single greatest recruiting class that college basketball had ever seen. So what did coach Steve Fisher do? He performed, in my mind, one of the greatest coaching jobs ever: he let them play. Certainly, he didn't just roll the ball onto the court and say, "OK, boys. Take me to the Final Four — two times," but you can bet that it was pretty close to that. Fisher recognized the talent in front of him, and rather than impeding that talent, or the individuality that usually accompanies such talent — in the Fab Five's case, the black socks, the shaved heads, and the ultra-baggy shorts — he allowed it to blossom, indeed reaching the national championship game in both 1992 and 1993.

Now, the "justification of paycheck" coach is of the exact opposite mentality. He feels he must "justify" his salary because he receives a "paycheck" to coach. Therefore, a lot of coaches invent a lot of theories and drills to make it look as though they are coaching when all they really need to do is to hone the natural skills that their players already possess. Jim Leyland, former Pirates, Marlins, and Rockies manager, said, "What the hell can I possibly tell Gary Sheffield about hitting? I was a career .220 *minor* league hitter." All he needed to do was make sure that Sheffield received his daily batting practice or perhaps have a brief chat with him from time to time about his life away from the field.

But what if Sheffield had been subjected to intrusive coaching? A poor coach might have screwed up Sheffield so badly with a bunch of ham-and-egg theories that Sheffield wouldn't know whether to jump or go blind. I know at least one hitter, Mark, who was badly affected in this way. "The best way to waste talent is to mis- or overcoach it," he told me. He was subtly referring to himself, a top high school baseball prospect who suffered through four miserable years of college due to his coach's incessant micromanaging.

Even professional baseball has similar situations. When I was with the Diamondbacks, we had a strength and conditioning coach who would appear at our minor league stadium from time to time. Whenever he came to town, we players would let out a collective groan because his arrival meant a series of pointless exercises. The coach was receiving a paycheck to make us bigger, stronger, faster, and better-conditioned athletes, which is fine during the offseason. During the season, though, sporadic exercising isn't going to do any good. In fact, when the coach showed up one day after having won eight games in a row, our director of player development joked, "Man, get the hell out of here; you never mess with a winning streak."

The ultimate weapon

So the question is, "How do you, the young aspiring ballplayer, deal with these types of coaches?" I can answer that in one word: diplomacy. I've had countless married men tell that the five most important words in a marriage are "Sorry, dear. You were right." If that's not diplomacy, I don't know what is. You must use the same bite-your-tongue, swallow-your-pride attitude when dealing with these types of coaches. Whether you like it or not — and whether it's fair or not — they have a major say in your career. One negative label getting around the baseball circles may be all it takes to brand you forever. All it takes is one argument with one coach to spread like wildfire in the baseball coaching fraternity. All it takes is one coach's assessment of you — lazy, smart-mouthed, cocky — to alter your baseball future forever. The worst part is that the label itself may not even be justified, and you may never get the chance to dispel it.

From a personal standpoint, if I had listened to every bit of advice that I've received over the years about hitting, I wouldn't even know how to hold the bat properly. As an extremely stubborn and, at times, hard-headed individual, I had to learn to acquiesce to the teachings of many of my coaches. I learned to say, "Yes, coach, I understand," and as soon as he turned his head, I would practice *my* way. You see, coaches, like almost all men in a position of authority, need to have their egos massaged. The last thing a coach needs is some know-it-all kid defying the very authority that he has worked so hard to attain.

Along these lines, most coaches fall subject to the "Success has a thousand fathers; failure is an orphan" way of thinking. What that means is if a coach has a player who reaches the big leagues, the coach will want to take a certain amount of credit for his player's success when, in fact, the coach may have had little or no impact on the player. It's easy for a coach to stick out his chest and boast, "Yep, I taught Johnnie everything he knows," but you will never hear a coach say, "You know, that Billy sure had a lot of talent, but I ruined him physically and psychologically."

Too many coaches, when they field a winning and successful team, want to receive all the credit for teaching their players their "system" of hitting, fielding, and baserunning. But there is one problem with that line of thinking. In baseball, systems don't win games; good players executing properly do. In football and basketball (I don't compare baseball to these sports to detract from them but to illustrate the skill vs. raw athleticism/emotion factor that exists) new offensive and defensive systems appear all the time and force other coaches to adjust accordingly. For example, in the 1980s and early 1990s, the "run and shoot" offense was the new wave in football offensive attacks. Even though Mouse Davis's brainchild lasted in the NFL for only a decade or so, it still afforded the teams that used it—specifically the Houston Oilers and Detroit Lions—a reasonable amount of success for a short time. In the NBA head coach Phil Jackson instituted Tex Winters' "triangle offense" to both the Michael Jordan–led Chicago Bulls and Shaquille O'Neal–led Los Angeles Lakers, and the system proved to be the final piece in each team's march to the multiple championships.

In baseball, however, there is no landscape-altering "system." There never has been, and there never will be. You never hear of a major league manager watching hour after hour of film like NFL coaches do. Baseball, or, more specifically, how to play winning baseball, was figured out 100 years ago, and it hasn't changed: pitching, defense, and timely hitting. Oh, sure, some managers prefer "small ball," which incorporates a lot of bunts and hit-and-runs while other managers, Earl Weaver for one, opt for the "pitching, defense, and three-run homers" strategy. Whatever the case, all a manager can do is field the best players available to him and let them do their jobs.

Finally, think of the movie *All the Right Moves*, where Tom Cruise plays a star high school football player and Craig T. Nelson plays an egomaniacal coach. Cruise's character, Stefan Djordjevic, is hoping to parlay his athletic prowess into a football scholarship, which will give him the education he so desperately needs to escape a life of toil in the dreaded steel mills of his hometown. Djordjevic, though, is extremely stubborn and constantly butts heads with the coach, causing the coach to throw Djordjevic off the team for insubordination and forcing him to spend his afternoons working in the mill rather than practicing on the football field.

Eventually, Djordjevic apologizes and the coach relents, and it makes for a happy ending, as Djordjevic gets the scholarship he so badly craved. My point is that to make your dreams come true, you will also have to make "all the right moves." This entire book is premised on the fact that you must control everything you can control, and one of those things is your attitude. Can you deal with coaches, and, more specifically, their egos? To do so, you will have to swallow your pride and your own ego at times. It may not be easy — it sure as heck wasn't for me — but it all comes down to one question: how badly do you want to play professional baseball?

13

The Draft

The draft. Is there a prouder moment in a ballplayer's life than when he can tell his friends and family that he was drafted? It is a watershed moment in an athlete's career, a moment that is a tangible reward for all the hard work and sacrifice up to that point. Each June, scores of quality amateur ballplayers sit by the phone hoping to get "the call." There is a lot of mystery involved with the draft, and I was personally misled by a newspaper article written about me in the winter of my junior year of high school.

The author of the article, which was written to praise and recognize me for being a top-notch student and four-sport athlete, included the comment that I "could be selected in the top five rounds of the draft" after my senior year. Later, he interviewed my baseball coach, who concurred with the author. As a 17-year-old, four-sport athlete who knew next to nothing about baseball except how to play it, I was thrilled. I didn't know I was that good. I figured that the spring and summer baseball seasons of 1989 had shown me to be a darn good ballplayer and that I was ready for professional baseball. As it turned out, not only was I not drafted a year later, I was *never* drafted. I didn't know that scouts looked for speed, arm strength and bat speed in high school players. I had none of these. I was a good high school baseball player in western Pennsylvania. Period. Pro ball? Forget about it. So you don't have to wander into the same abyss that I did, I included this chapter about Major League Baseball Free Agent Draft.

Why aren't the scouts looking at me?

The frustrating part of amateur baseball is that the players who produce on the field are often the ones who are repeatedly passed over for the draft. I experienced it all through college, and I didn't like a whole lot. I thought, "I'll show those bastards that I'm better than all these guys the scouts like." It was extremely difficult for me, as a quixotic college student, to accept the fact that despite my good numbers, no one wanted to draft me. You may be experiencing the same phenomenon right now as you watch the scouts flock to see a statistically inferior teammate or opponent. To come to grips with this reality, you must first understand that there are two types of ballplayers who are drafted: the "potential" player and the "polished" player.

The potential player is the player who has one or two or three outstanding tools, either as a pitcher or as a hitter. As an example, take a high school position player. He has blazing speed — yet no idea how to steal a base or track down a fly ball. He has a rocket for an arm — yet no idea where the ball is going. He has a body chiseled out of marble — yet his swing is as smooth as a rusty gate and results in a .250 batting average. So why do all the scouts drool over him? Well, they see a mountain of potential. They don't look at his baseball skill now; they picture him five years from now, after five seasons of professional baseball. It may not make sense to you, but the player who can't even make the All-Section team in high school may end his senior season with a six-figure signing bonus.

The polished player is the type of player who performs well at each level and has neither an eye-popping strength nor a glaring weakness. He has proven that he can hit or pitch at the previous level and therefore deserves a shot at the next. Unfortunately, a lot of these players never get a chance to prove themselves at that next level of play. Particularly at the professional level, scouts and player personnel people will determine, rightly or wrongly, that a certain player has "maxed out" his potential, and just as the brass licks its chops when it pictures the potential player in five years, it rolls its eyes when envisioning the polished player. In fact, it can be as cut-and-dry as a simple question: Can we see this player playing in the big leagues? Apparently, that was the question that circulated around the meeting room of the Arizona Diamondbacks in the fall of 1997 (according to an insider's reports). When the player in question was one Bo Durkac, the consensus was that the brass could not. I was given my release papers shortly thereafter.

I can still remember the following scene as if it were yesterday: during the early part of my junior year of college, we were in a tournament in Florida. I had just come off a sophomore season having hit .423 (good for 21st in the country) and a subsequent summer wooden-bat league (the Northeast Collegiate Baseball League, in upstate New York) where I hit .350. Our catcher, on the other hand, was an average college hitter at best — he ended up hitting about .260 that season — yet a representative from the Major League Scouting Bureau (an organization that keeps a large database of potential professional prospects) was videotaping *him* during batting practice and not me. It's funny, looking back, how bitter and shortchanged I felt about the ordeal, but now, eight years later, I understand perfectly. To borrow a line from the movie *Top Gun,* "It takes a lot more than fancy flying."

At the time, I didn't understand that scouts don't look only at statistics; oftentimes, stats are the *last* thing scouts consider. Our catcher had played in the prestigious Cape Cod League, where he was selected as an alternate to the All-Star team, during the previous summer and was considered a top-notch, if undersized, defensive catcher. (His size — he was about 5'10" tall and weighed about 200 lbs.— kept him from being an extremely desired commodity, prompting him to say during that tournament, which featured a team with a 6'4", 220 lbs. catcher, "Jeez, Bo, if I was that big, I wouldn't go to class again for the rest of the year.")

The four "defensive" positions on the field are catcher, shortstop, second base, and centerfield, and the ability to play well defensively at these positions is more important than offensive numbers. Any productivity that one of these defensive players can provide with the bat is considered "icing on the cake." It didn't matter to a Los Angeles Dodgers scout that our catcher didn't hit too well; he liked his defensive ability. The Dodgers offered him a free agent contract after the draft, our catcher accepted, and played Rookie league for the Dodgers that summer. I, unfortunately, had to return to the same collegiate league, stewing about the "oversight" all summer long.

I felt slighted, to be sure, but what could I do? Once again, I used the snub as motivation for my upcoming senior season. I mentioned my "weight problem" and how I gave up alcoholic beverages in an effort to shed unwanted pounds. During my junior year, one scout, Ron Elam, of the Oakland A's, came to see a game against James Madison University — a game in which I hit two homeruns and a triple — and I remember his making a comment about my portliness, saying something like, "You might be able to play offensive line for the (Washington) Redskins with that build." Being the stubborn ass that I was back then, I thought, "So what if he thinks I'm fat? I can *play,* and I'm good enough that someone will draft me." Boy, was I wrong about that.

Later that summer, during the NCBL All-Star game, a scout mentioned to my mom that I didn't look "explosive." Reading between the lines, he was saying that I was fat, and, reading further, that scouts don't usually draft pudgy, non-homerun hitting third basemen. The writing on the wall then became crystal clear: get a better body or forget about playing pro ball. For the 347th time, you have to control what you can control, especially when you are a polished player like I was. When you possess tons of natural ability, a scout will say, "Yes, maybe he is a bit overweight, but our strength and conditioning program will take care of that." When you're a "what you see is what you get" player, however, being ten pounds overweight is a major hindrance to your draftability.

The baseball draft, although less magnified, is no different from the NFL Draft or from a beauty pageant: the powers-that-be determine what they want you to look like, and if you want the position badly enough, you will conform to their wishes. Image is everything, and just as pro football teams never draft short, slow, old men and beauty pageants never crown old, obese women, amateur baseball players are expected to look the part. No, you don't have to look like Arnold Schwarzenegger, but you can't look like Danny DeVito, either. Part of being "draftable" is your appearance. Work on that as much as you work on your pitching, hitting, and fielding.

For the high school student

It almost seems pointless to include a chapter about the draft because only high school players with a lot of natural ability are drafted. Players with a lot of natural ability don't tend to read books entitled *How to Become a Professional Baseball Player*. Books like this one are generally reserved for the "blue-collar" ballplayers or the "students of the game." It is possible, however, for the potential ballplayer to be a "thinking" ballplayer and for the polished player to turn himself into a draftable commodity.

Here's a fact: major league organizations will only draft a high school position player who can run extremely well and who can throw pretty well or a pitcher who can throw over 90 MPH. No, that's not true 100 percent of the time, but pretty close. Organizations look for these traits because they can't be taught, with the thinking that they can, in fact, teach a position player how to hit and field; they feel they can teach a pitcher how to spot his fastball and throw a decent breaking ball and changeup. Scouts have sought these qualities in young players for 100 years and will continue to look for them for the next 100 years. About the only time a scout will draft a player who can't run is when he is a corner infielder (first or third baseman) or a catcher who can really hit well and who possesses a strong throwing arm.

Another reason why they look for these traits is for a back-up plan. Did you know that both Mickey Mantle and Willie Mays were originally signed as shortstops? Obviously, at some point early in their professional careers, the two of them struggled defensively at shortstop or else they would have never been converted to the outfield. Because the speed and the arm strength of these two men are stuff of legend, they developed into two of the greatest defensive centerfielders of all time. Their successful change of position would not have been possible, though, without the two tools they possessed naturally.

Believe it or not, a lot of major leaguers began their careers at positions other than the ones they currently play. In order to change positions, however, a player must possess the required tools to play the new position. That's the other reason why speed and arm strength are such highly regarded commodities: you need one or both at virtually every position on the field. If an organization drafts a player, invests a lot of money in him, and then decides three years later that his current position is not working out, they try him at a new position. Usually, that means moving an infielder to the outfield, where speed and arm strength are hugely important.

From a pitching standpoint, in today's day and age, it is extremely rare for an organization to draft a pitcher — especially a righty — who doesn't throw at least 90 MPH. That's just the way the baseball minds think nowadays. In fact, our pitching coach when I played for the Chico (CA) Heat, Jeff Pico, was selected in the 13th round out of high school in 1984 by the Chicago Cubs, and he estimates that his fastball was roughly 85 MPH back then. We both agree that if he were the same pitcher in 2002, he may not even be drafted at all, let alone in the 13th round. Just as organizations look to shape and mold raw talent into polished, complete position players, they also look to put the harnesses on a young arm, teach him some control, and introduce him to a few new pitches for his repertoire. Everything starts with the fastball, and the pitcher who can combine a solid fastball with control and some offspeed pitches will generally have some success. Conversely, if a pitcher has a nice breaking pitch and changeup but not a fastball to set them up, the scouts feel that good hitters will have little problem adjusting to the soft stuff when there is little fear of the fastball. This type of pitcher usually has to prove himself at the upper echelon of college baseball for him to get a chance to play professionally.

For the college student

In college players, scouts tend to look for a combination of polished and potential talent for one simple reason: The time the player has spent in college is time he could have spent with an organization. No organization wants to take a guy with two years of college experience and keep him in the minors for five years in order to develop into a big leaguer. He would reach the big leagues at roughly 25-years-old, a little older than what the organization would like. (If the organization drafts a player out of high school, however, they usually have no problem with a five-year plan.) In return for his one, two or three years of college baseball, an organization would expect a certain amount of "polish" on a college player.

Typically, though, organizations prefer the potential player to the polished one. At the ages of 19, 20, and 21, most organizations feel they can teach the game to a sufficiently talented young player, but a 22- or 23-year-old is probably at his ceiling from an ability standpoint. In other words, if you haven't shown the ability to play baseball at a major-league level by that age, you will never learn. As you'll see in the next section, if you're a "polished" player and you have one bad year, you may get your walking papers. The way an organization looks at it is you get one chance each year to prove your worth. If you fail to produce, then your job will probably go to a potential player, someone who needs as many at-bats or innings pitched as possible to develop into a major leaguer.

Should I stay or should I go?

There are numerous arguments in favor of the high school student's bypassing college and going directly to the professional ranks. There are numerous arguments in favor of the college (or junior college) student's leaving school early to pursue his major league aspirations. But there are also many valid reasons to attend — or to stay in — college. I do not have an overwhelming opinion on which way is the "correct" way to go, and therefore all I can do is provide you with the facts, and here they are.

The Advantages of Skipping College

One big advantage of going directly to the pros is that you will be immersed into the cold, hard world of professional baseball. You will learn how to deal with the rigors of a 140-game season, long bus trips, and how to stretch $15 over three meals in one day. Also, you will receive hour upon hour of instruction; the time limits that restrict college coaching do not pertain to pro baseball. As a hitter, you will begin hitting with a wooden bat at 18-years-old. A lot of hitters never figure out how to make the transition from the aluminum of college to the wood of the pros, so the sooner you can start the process, the better off you'll be. As a pitcher, you don't have to worry about being overpitched by some egomaniacal college coach who cares more about his win-loss record than he does about the health of your arm. The Pitching Coordinator of your organization will see to it that you receive ample instruction without endangering the well-being of your arm. All of these are solid reasons to go pro, but the biggest reason is what follows: money.

As I mentioned earlier, if a scout drafts you out of high school, then you probably possess some pretty quality tools. The more tools you have, the more patience an organization will exercise when determining your worth. Furthermore, the more tools you have, the more money the organization will invest in you, and your signing bonus, more than anything, becomes the best indicator of how long it will keep you around.

Along these lines, this could be a typical conversation between a General Manager and a Director of Player Development:

> DPD: "You know, ol' Johnny Jones isn't really doing anything in his fourth year of A ball. I'm thinking of releasing him."
> GM: "Well, we drafted him in the second round five years ago and gave him $1.4 million because he has a ton of raw ability. Why haven't you guys been able to teach him how to hit or to play third base?"
> DPD: "Believe me, we've tried, but the kid just doesn't have any baseball instincts. He has no idea how to hit the curveball, and he's good for an error — usually a throwing one — every other game. On top of it all, his manager tells me that he likes to go out a lot at night and has missed the team bus twice this year."
> GM: "I see. I wish I could say that we overdrafted him, but do you want to go to Mr. Owner and tell him that we gave this kid $1.4 million and still missed on him?"
> DPD: "Not really."
> GM: "Me neither. Let's keep him around for two more years, and he hasn't shown any progress by then, we'll get rid of him."

If Johnny Jones were a polished player, he would receive one or two years in Class A to prove himself. One bad year usually means his release. In the minor leagues, sometimes you just have to outlast your competition. You need to do whatever it takes to keep an affiliated uniform on your back. If that means milking an organization for every penny to have them keep you around for a few extra years, then do it. Certainly, as a high school player, you have the most leverage of any point in your career. Chances are that if a scout is seriously considering drafting you, then the colleges probably aren't too far behind in their recruitment of you. (Remember what I said about the importance of good grades? A scholarship offer to an expensive private school can mean as much as one hundred thousand dollars in bargaining power with an organization, but there may be no scholarship offer if you have lousy grades.) The money, and the subsequent commitment to you by the organization, is perhaps the greatest reason to bypass college.

The Advantages of Going to College

When you're young, talented, and full of confidence and desire, you never picture *not* making it to the big leagues. You don't see yourself eight years down the line saying, "Jeez, I gave baseball everything I had, and I have nothing to show for it. Not a lot of money. No college education. No real-world training." Unfortunately, the majority of professional players end up in this situation, and they find themselves having to start from scratch at the age of 26 or 28. Many players, by this point in their careers, have married and have probably started a family. Therefore, because of the litany of bills they face each month, they are financially unable to attend college, and they are forced into a life of temporary and dead-end jobs.

If, however, you attend college — even if it's only for two or three years — at least you have a head start on life after baseball. By not signing a pro contract out of high school, you will be forfeiting tens of thousands of dollars in the short run, but by choosing to attend college, you are making a back-up plan — and you can *still* be drafted and *still* get a modest signing bonus down the road.

Finally, in three words, *college is awesome.* When I say college, I mean the entire college experience. I wouldn't have traded my four-and-a-half years for anything else in the world. I received an education, met a lot of great guys and girls, matured physically and socially, and, oh yeah, I got to play major college baseball. If you, as a high school senior, were drafted, then you obviously have some ability. Ability doesn't just disappear, barring a major injury, of course. Assuming you don't sit on your ass for four years of college, you should receive the opportunity to play professionally. No, you won't receive the same signing bonus as a senior in college as would have received had you signed after high school, but the trade-off, in my eyes, is equivalent. You simply can't put a price on experiences and life. Unless your signing bonus is so substantial — usually for players selected in the first three rounds— that it is virtually impossible to pass up, I wholeheartedly recommend going to college.

For the College Student

Once again, baseball is a business, and the more money you can squeeze out of an organization, the longer it will keep you around. Perhaps in that one extra season the organization holds on to you, you may have your breakout year and all of a sudden find yourself on a fast track to the big leagues. In order to get top dollar, you need bargaining power, and every year of college eligibility you have left is more power at the negotiation table.

As a junior college (juco) player, the key is to sign a National Letter of Intent (the college version of a contract) with the best school — and for the most amount of scholarship money — possible. If you can tell the scout who drafts you, "Well, I just signed with the defending national champs for a full scholarship, and my parents and I think it's a good idea to get my education," then your scout is between a rock and a hard place if he is serious about signing you. If, however, you don't have any post-juco plans, then he has *you* behind the eight ball. (Do I really need to make another "the importance of education" analogy?)

If you attend a four-year college, then unless you turn 21 within 45 days of the draft of your sophomore season, you are not draftable until your junior season. Generally, when discussing the pro ball vs. college issue, I am an advocate of going the college route. As a college junior, though, I recommend that you take the money and run. It's simply about opportunity cost. Signing after your junior year usually means a far greater signing bonus because you have that last year of eligibility as the final ace in the hole in the bargaining process. In my opinion, the enlarged signing bonus far outweighs the one year of education you are forsaking. You can always go back to college for that one last year of education.

Agents

Let's say, in a best-case scenario, you have become quite the college baseball player by the end of your sophomore year. Let's say you go off to the Cape Cod League where you are among the top players in the league and scouts start scribbling furiously in their notepads whenever you're on the field. The chances of your being drafted next spring appear to be excellent. Now, let's say that it is not question of *if* you'll be drafted, but *when*. During the early spring of your junior year, scouts call you to say that they want to select you between the third and fifth rounds, and, even better, guys named Scott Boras and Jeff Moorad — two of the premier agents in sports — begin courting you. All of a sudden, dollar signs begin dancing in your head, and you don't know what to do.

First of all, relax. If you're that good that scouts and agents are pestering you, then you'll get what you're entitled to. Secondly, immediately — and I mean *immediately* — consult your college's compliance representative. Most schools have someone on staff specifically for NCAA rules interpretations, and he or she will be well versed on your rights as a student-athlete. The rules regarding agent-athlete relations seem to be constantly changing, and it is in your best interest, financially and in terms of your eligibility, to proceed cautiously. I do know that you *cannot* sign a contract with an agent and still maintain your eligibility. I believe you can speak with an agent, but, once again, be sure to contact your compliance representative at the first hint of agent contact.

Finally, I will not purport to know what's best for you and your family. I have heard stories, however, of high-round draft picks holding out for a ton of money when the offers on the table are only a few pounds short of a ton. There is a story of a player who, in a recent draft, demanded a $4.5 million signing bonus from a team that said it would go no higher than $4 million. Negotiations stalled, the organization decided to go a different direction, and the player was left with nothing. Average ballplayers all over the country collectively cringed. I have to think of the old saying, "A great plan today is better than a perfect plan tomorrow." Enough said.

14

For the Parents

One thing that never ceases to amaze me is the amount of money that parents will spend on their children. Whether it's springing for academic tutoring, piano lessons, ballet, or baseball instruction, all parents seem to want the best for their children. Certainly, I, as an unmarried, childless 30-year-old, am not qualified to speak on proper parenting, but any time parents put whatever money is left over at the of the month towards their children's futures—as opposed to that new sports car Dad has been eyeing—it has to be a good thing. There is one question, though, that begs asking: Are the parents hoping to enhance the child's participation and enjoyment in his or her activity, or are they trying to force the child into a life of fame and riches that they themselves could never attain? In other words, are the parents living vicariously through their children or, even worse, hoping to ride the wave of fortune that their children may one day find?

Tiger Woods is perhaps the premier athlete on the planet right now, and his relationship with his father is well documented. According to Earl (the father), he never had to push Tiger to the golf course. Tiger's fanatical desire to play golf came from deep within the youngster, and, in my opinion, that's fine. Unfortunately, no one ever documents the antithesis of the Woods' relationship. Sure, every so often, a Todd Marinovich pops up on the sports scene, but what about the high school kid who ends up hating his father because of the father's overbearing presence in the child's sports-related life? You know what I mean. You see those fathers at sporting events and you mumble to yourself, "Boy, I feel so bad for little Johnnie out there." Little Johnnie, as soon as he makes some form of a mistake on the field or court or rink, immediately looks in the stands to see the expression on his father's face. Little Johnnie feels not the pressure of the contest, but that of his dad.

Heck, I *played* with kids like that in high school, and I truly felt sorry for them.

Because my father played major college basketball, he never felt compelled to push sports on my siblings or me. Oh, sure, he was a little bit disappointed that none of us chose basketball as our #1 sport — my brother and I started playing hockey at the tender ages of three and five, respectively, and hockey was much more the *en vogue* sport in Western Pennsylvania in the 1980s — but he got over it. He and my mother were extremely supportive parents, but not once did I ever feel as though they were force-feeding me sports. In fact, when I was in high school and playing four sports, some parents would ask my parents if they feared my burning out of sports, and they would just chuckle and shake their heads and tell them that it was all my decision.

A good friend of mine once said to me, "Every dad thinks his kid is the next Mickey Mantle." I suppose there is some truth to that statement. I mean, have you ever heard a parent say, "Boy, my kid is just a big screw-up?" Not likely. It's one thing to encourage a child toward the world of sports, and, more specifically, toward baseball; it's another — and detrimental — thing to ram it down his throat.

In this chapter I do not wish to paint a grim picture about the world of amateur and professional baseball. As the consummate realist, I simply want you to be informed as you guide your child down the path of amateur athletics. The road is filled with potholes, speed bumps, and terrible drivers, but as long as you and your son maneuver as carefully as possible in search of your destination, it can be a fun rewarding trip for everyone involved.

Be logical

If there are currently 30 major league teams and each team carries 25 players, you don't have to be a genius to figure that at any one time, there are only 750 active major leaguers. In the entire world of almost six billion people, only 750 athletes can call themselves "big leaguers." Obviously, only a fraction of the population of the earth produces baseball players — I am not aware of any major leaguers from the Belgian Congo — but you get my point: the odds of reaching The Show are remote at best.

Now, let's say the average major league organization has roughly 175 players (three Rookie-level teams, two Class A teams, one AA team and one AAA team; each team would carry 25 players) under contract at any given time. The total number of minor leaguers (independent leagues excluded) in the world, therefore, would total 5250. So, if my math is correct, one out every eight minor leaguers will reach the big leagues. That ratio doesn't seem too steep, does it? But wait. This book is designed to get your son from amateur baseball to professional baseball—which is much more difficult, statistically, than going from the minors to the majors—so let's look at the amateur ranks.

According to the NCAA, at the time of this book's printing, there are 863 college baseball programs in the country, all three divisions included. Since only juniors and seniors are draft-eligible and comprise roughly half of a 25-man roster, I did the following computation:

863 programs × 13 draft-eligible players per team = 11,219 draft-eligible players

Using the same formula for the National Junior College Athletic Association (in which *every* player is draft-eligible) and the National Association of Intercollegiate Athletics, I came up with the following statistics:

NJCAA — 387 teams
387 × 25 = 9675

NAIA — 232 teams
232 × 13 = 3016

Therefore, in any given year, a total of 23,910 college baseball players are draft-eligible. But wait; it gets worse. According to the National Federation of State High School Associations, in 2001, 450,513 boys played high school baseball. Since only seniors are draft-eligible and tend to make up, in my opinion, one-third of a high school team, I did the math again:

450,513 / 3 = 150,171

Now, taking the totals for the collegiate and prep athletes, you can see that baseball scouts have 174,081 players to choose from on draft day. Each team has 50 selections, make a grand total of 1500 draft choices in any one draft. (Some organizations will offer "free agent" contracts to fringe players rather than actually draft them. The total number of these players in a given year is negligible compared to those whom are drafted.) When all of the math is said and done, your draft-eligible son has 0.86 percent chance of being drafted. Or, rounding conservatively, he has a 1 in 100 chance of playing professional baseball. The odds are simply not in his favor. (At the time this book went to print, Major League Baseball was considering a "world-wide" draft. In the past, players not born in the USA, Canada, or Puerto Rico were able to sign as a free agent with whatever team they chose. Under this proposed legislation, every player in the world would fall subject to the same draft, further reducing the odds of your son's being drafted.)

Does that mean he should throw in the towel and concentrate solely on his schoolwork or on another sport? Absolutely not. Being part of a college baseball team is wonderful. Rather than joining a fraternity, he will immediately have a brotherhood with his teammates. Some players will join the team each year, and some will leave. He will get along with some players, and he will not get along with others. He will keep in touch with some of them for the rest of his life, and he will never again speak to others. To me, developing socially is an integral part of the whole college process, and as a member of the baseball team — as opposed to a normal college student — he will form an instant bond that will help him with the transitional difficulties that most freshman face.

Most importantly, though, he will have a goal. Is his goal playing professional baseball? Perhaps. Does he have a realistic shot at it? Probably not, but you never know. Maybe his goal is to go to the College World Series, be it at the Division I level or at the NAIA level. Whatever the case, he will be working towards something rather than drifting through his matriculation with no purpose other than getting a college diploma. Many collegiate athletes perform much better academically during their in-seasons than their off-seasons because of the rigorous game and practice schedule involved; that schedule, along with eating, sleeping, going to class, and doing homework, eliminates a lot of free time that many college students use unwisely.

Don't be discouraged by the odds. Your son can have a fun-filled, rewarding collegiate baseball career and get his diploma. If he develops enough from a talent standpoint to enter into professional baseball, then so be it. If not, though, he'll know he gave it his best shot, received an education, and made some lifelong friends.

Transferring

When I was in high school, I always followed the progress of the older players in my area who would go off to play college baseball. Naturally, I was comparing myself to those players to determine what my own future in baseball would be. Not too many players whom I can recall ever went very far away for college, and of the ones who did, many of them transferred to colleges closer to home. Whenever I read about the returning ballplayer, I always thought to myself, "Jeez, what a wimp this guy must be! He couldn't hack it being away from Mommy and Daddy, so he had to come home." Little did I know that I, though not for exactly the same reasons, would be in the same position after one year of college.

The decision to transfer colleges is usually more stressful than choosing your original destination. For one, your son's dreams of playing college baseball have been shattered — temporarily — by his current college coach, who has undoubtedly made it clear that he will receive little or no playing time in the future, or, worse yet, that he is no longer welcome on his team. Secondly, once he has decided to transfer, he will have only two or three months to find a new school, and a lot of schools already have their fall rosters set by mid-summer. If that is the case, he may find himself as a "preferred walk-on," someone the coaches may have seen play and may like but is not worthy of a scholarship. Although he isn't a walk-on in the truest sense (someone whom the coaches have never seen before), he isn't necessarily part of the team, either. And even if your son is worthy of a scholarship, there simply may not be any scholarship money left by the middle of summer.

When I transferred to Virginia Tech in the fall of 1992, I distinctly remember walking around campus thinking, "Jeez, this the second straight fall that I've had to start at a college of 20,000+ students without knowing a soul. The sacrifice better be worth it." I was alone, frustrated with having to meet a whole new group of ballplayers again, and in doubt of my own baseball ability after a lousy four weeks of fall practice. Somehow, I was able to summon enough intestinal fortitude to get me through to the spring, when I finally tasted some success.

As painful and traumatic as transferring can be, however, it beats the alternative: no baseball. Sure, it would have been easy for someone to stay at UNC. It's a great academic institution with world-renowned athletics on a beautiful campus. Most people would kill to have a chance to attend and receive a diploma from UNC, but I wasn't one of those people. College without baseball would have been like a day without oxygen. I didn't care about what I was leaving; I cared only about what I would be missing. Sorry, but I had dreams.

Does your son have that love of the game? Is he willing to put his future on hold while he chases a seemingly unattainable goal? If not, then, assuming he's happy where he is, perhaps he shouldn't transfer. When something grabs hold of your heart and won't let go, logic and reason often take a backseat to its pursuit. As a hungry, sacrifice-at-all-costs young ballplayer, I would have done *anything* to play college baseball. I hope you and your son can find his ideal institution right out of high school and that you never have to deal with the transfer process, but if you do, just present your son with his options and allow his heart to make the decision.

Can you, the parents, deal with the adversity?

When I was a junior in college, I slumped to a .278 batting average. That may not sound too shabby, but having hit .423 the previous spring, I was positively devastated. I was convinced that I had what it took to be drafted, but I certainly wasn't going anywhere with that lousy number. After one particular home game against Virginia Commonwealth, I grounded out weakly to end the game, and as I was doing my running in the outfield after the contest, I was crying my eyes out. I was so frustrated that I didn't know what to do. My ultra-supportive parents had driven the six hours to Blacksburg for the weekend, and I could barely utter a word to them on the way home from the field.

We returned to my apartment, and as I was visiting with my roommates, my mom snuck upstairs to my room. When I went up there to change clothes, I found her reading Ted Williams's *The Science of Hitting*, my "bible," if you will. She knew what kind of agony I was going through, and she was suffering from it as well. After that evening's dinner filled with their questions and my monosyllabic answers, she went to bed in the hotel and had a dream about me hitting one of my textbook base-hits, a line drive over shortstop. Like something out of fictional baseball story, I did exactly that the next day, and before long, I was hitting .330 again.

If you are the type of parents like my mom, be prepared for a lot of heartache in your and your son's lives. I've already told you about how the numbers are severely stacked against your son's making it to professional baseball, but another harsh reality is this: there are a lot of other obstacles along the way.

One form of adversity that existed in my days in small doses but is now out of control is the politics involved in amateur sports. I suppose all the stories you hear about fathers assaulting umpires and other fathers is merely an extension of my suggestion earlier that too many parents are looking for their own personal improvements through the athletic success of their children. It's one thing to want the best for your child; it's another thing to let that desire turn you into a Jekyll-and-Hyde persona.

It seems as though politics rears its ugly head in everything from choosing coaches for a Little League All-Star team to choosing the players for that same team. Can you, as a loving, well-intentioned parent, be objective enough to say, "You know, Johnnie is a damn good ballplayer, but he's just not quite good enough to make the All-Star team"? Can you deal with the parents who don't share your objectivity? It may not be easy, but if you can set a positive example with your attitude, perhaps others will follow and everyone—especially the kids—will benefit. Think about it: Is your son's selection to the Little League All-Star really that important in the big picture? It may seem to be, but believe me, if your son is good enough and dedicated enough, a lot of those kids who were selected in front of him will fall by the wayside by the time he reaches high school. At that point, the cream will rise to the top.

Can you handle it financially?

Playing amateur sports is definitely not cheap. Some sports, like soccer, require extensive travel (I have a second cousin who is goalie at a Division I school in the Midwest, and I remember how many miles she and her family traveled over the course of her travel team days). Others, like hockey, require both heavy traveling *and* expensive equipment. In fact, I recall that during my pre-teen days, several of my hockey-playing friends were on the verge of being unable to play each year due to the financial strain the sport put on their families.

As your son enters his teenage years, when the weeding out process begins, your son will begin to compete for travel teams. Perhaps the biggest key to playing professional baseball is to get to the best baseball college possible, and the key to reaching that goal is exposure. Unlike in the professional ranks, colleges don't have a scouting department, *per se*. Yes, the top 30 or so programs in the college baseball world have greater funds at their disposal than the others and can therefore spend a little more money on the recruiting process, but it's just not financially feasible for a coach to travel all over the country looking for ballplayers. So, coaches flock to these talent-laden camps and tournaments to evaluate the young athletes. Obviously, if your son has designs on playing collegiately — at the highest level possible in accordance to his ability — he needs to make his local travel team.

Because "travel" is the operative word in travel team, you, as parents, need to finance your son's travels. Certainly, fundraisers can help out, but can you make up the difference? Whether it's paying for gasoline, hotel rooms, meals, equipment, or — in case of emergencies — hospital costs or car troubles, your checking account will most likely be under duress. Naturally, the parents must discuss with each other the financial ramifications of letting your son join a travel team, but I will say this about it: If you foresee financial difficulties, I think it is better to keep your son off the team than it is to let him join and then pull him off it. Once he gets a taste of facing good competition and performing in front of college and pro scouts, removing him from the limelight might be traumatic. In other words, what he doesn't know won't hurt him.

Finally, once your son reaches the college ranks, he may have the option of playing in a summer collegiate league. There are several of them around the country — the Cape Cod League and the Alaskan League are the two most prominent — and the competition, outside of these two leagues, is pretty similar. The reasons for playing in a collegiate league are two-fold: (1) To improve at baseball, your son needs to play as many games as possible in a year. Staying home for the summer and lifting weights or hitting off a tee or at the local batting cages won't help him nearly as much as playing will. (2) Exposure is critical. Now, when I say exposure, I don't mean just to professional scouts; if you're good enough, they'll find you. I mean showing your ability to other college coaches, because as much as I hate to be a pessimist, your son may find himself needing to transfer schools at some point. If he can make a good impression on his summer league coach, who is a college coach of some kind, your son may be able to use the coach for connections to other programs.

In these summer leagues, the players are given jobs to work during the day, but the pay is usually minimum wage. Oftentimes, but not all the time, players will stay with host families. If a player has to provide his own lodging, then he may find that a minimum-wage job doesn't exactly pay the bills. Also, he may have to pay for his travel to and from his destination. Playing in a summer league is critical, and although the player will have a source of income — albeit a minuscule one — he may have to lean on Mom and Dad for help.

As a parent, you want the best for your child. As the parent of an athlete, attaining that goal is a lot more difficult. Trying to console your 13-year-old daughter after a breakup with her "boyfriend" can be tough, but can you imagine having to nurture your son after his professional aspirations have been shattered? In the opening paragraph, I wrote that I didn't want to paint a grim picture about the pursuit of professional baseball, and I don't. However, I do want you to understand the number of setbacks your son will encounter along the way. I once read a quote by famed baseball author Roger Kahn, who said, "Implausible dreams are often the most passionate of all." Your son's dream of playing professional baseball — and, perhaps, major league baseball — may be somewhat implausible, but nothing ventured, nothing gained, right?

The question you must ask yourself is, in my opinion, "How serious is my son about baseball?" To answer it, ask yourself other questions. Does his every thought, action, and conversation revolve around baseball? Do I have to tell him to practice? Does he leap out of bed for an early morning workout, or do I have to drag him out of the house? Finally, do the flames of desire burn inside him? Without a raging inferno pushing him to excel, it is likely that he won't. You, as a parent, need to be able to recognize the presence — or absence — of that desire. If he doesn't have it, there is no point in backing him emotionally or financially while he chases his dreams.

To be sure, your son's chances of playing professional baseball are quite remote, but the journey can nevertheless be a lot of fun. I know my parents enjoyed visiting me during my college baseball seasons, and they made a lot of new friends in doing so. In my professional days in California, I know my father always looked forward to his vacation each summer to escape the hot and humid Pennsylvania weather and watch a week or two of games. He and my mother knew I probably that I wasn't going to the big leagues, but they still enjoyed visiting new parts of the country, meeting new people, and, of course, watching their son play baseball. They knew how badly I wanted this dream, and therefore, they had no problem with my chasing it. We enjoyed every minute of it. If your son is serious about it, then you can, too.

15

The World of Professional Baseball

I suppose I would be remiss if I didn't include a chapter on professional baseball. After all, the idea of this book is get you to that level, and by not giving you at least *some* insight as to what professional baseball is all about, I would feel as if I were shortchanging you. (I figure if Mike Schmidt can include a chapter for pitchers in his hitting book, I can include one about the path to the big leagues.) Without question, you have worked and slaved your way to get to professional baseball. You have made yourself into the best player you could become, sacrificed, dealt with all the politics, and kept your nose clean. By God, you have *earned* this opportunity. I have helped to prepare you for this moment, and now, I want to help you reach your ultimate goal — the big leagues.

I want to use this paragraph to offer a brief, preliminary commentary on professional baseball. I played minor league baseball for seven years, and I enjoyed *every single minute* of it. When I work with a kid, either as a tutor or as a coach, I always ask him, "Getting paid to play baseball — that's a pretty good deal, huh?" You should see his eyes light up. For seven years, I received a biweekly paycheck to play a sport. Pete Rose said that being paid to play baseball is like having a license to steal, and I concur. As cynical as I may sound from time to time about the world of baseball, make no mistake: I would not change my pro baseball experience for anything in the world. The journey, however, is not all peaches and cream, and thick skin is as much of a necessity as footspeed and arm strength. I don't mean to discourage you from your dreams; in fact, I seek the opposite result. I want you to understand that I am probably not much different from you, and if I could do it, so can

177

you. But I also want to make you aware of what pro baseball — the institution — is all about. After all, only a fool tests the depth of water with both feet.

A cruel, cruel world

The first thing you must realize is that professional baseball is a cutthroat, intensely competitive occupation. There is only one goal: the big leagues. The days of hanging out and partying together with all your teammates are over. For example, after the first game of my senior season at Virginia Tech (a Saturday night), I threw a party at my apartment for our baseball team. Of the 30 members of our team, I would guess that 27 showed up. Getting a 90 percent turnout for a professional team's party would be unheard of. With the vastly different types of players who must coexist on a minor league team, it is rare to have an entire team hang out as group. Most teams split up into groups based on similar interest and go their separate ways after games.

Also, while you're together at the park, don't expect everyone to get along and converse freely with each other. For one, there is the obvious language barrier, but, in addition, there is an omnipresent egotism/ethnocentrism factor involved. Most ballplayers are so wrapped up in themselves that they don't have time for the other players. Sure, every guy on a team will find one or two guys to hang out with, but rarely do players associate with guys from different interest groups. Heck, I've been on teams where a guy, other than congratulating him for a nice play on the field, didn't say more than ten words to another player *all year*. I have developed a certain disdain for the words "camaraderie" and "team chemistry" and their relevance in professional baseball. Well, you tell me: how can you expect to have any kind of team "togetherness" when certain players either cannot or, worse yet, choose not to talk to certain other players?

Now, here's the ultimate shocker about the attitudes of minor league ballplayers: no one really cares if the team wins or loses. Huh? Yes, it is true. The reason no one cares is that the minor leagues is all about player development, not wins and losses. Obviously, everyone likes to win, and when the team wins, usually — *usually*— everyone is happy. On the other hand, the only people who give a damn about a loss are the fans, the manager, and the one or two or three players who performed poorly that night and either did not help the team win or who caused the team to lose. When directors of player development evaluate the talent within their respective minor league systems, they look at, among other things, ERA's, batting averages, stolen bases, and fielding percentages; they could not care less about wins and losses of the teams. To illustrate this fact, let me tell you a story.

My first affiliated minor league team, the 1996 Visalia Oaks of the Class A California League, was a "co-op." A co-op means that there was more than one organization's ballplayers on the team. When we arrived in Visalia on April 1, the team consisted of two Minnesota Twins, eight Arizona Diamondbacks, and fifteen Detroit Tigers. Several of the Tigers told me of a low-level minor league team within the organization a few years earlier which had a record of something like 15–65, or maybe even worse than that. Pretty lousy, right? Well, within four years, five players off that team were in the big leagues. The percentages say that one player from a short-season Class A team will make it to the big leagues. To have *five* from one team is unfathomable. The brass decided that these supremely talented, yet skill-deprived players needed as much playing time as possible to develop. The brass understands that there is only one goal for an organization: to win the World Series. Developing talent within the organization is the best way to do that, and if that means playing these aforementioned potential players in front of the polished players at the expense of the team's win-loss record, so be it. Of course, if a team can win a championship while developing major league talent, the championship is the icing on the cake.

Finally, if you think the world of amateur baseball was unfair, wait until you get into pro baseball. Hypocrisy runs rampant throughout the minor leagues. If a first round draft pick has an upbeat and enthusiastic attitude, the brass gushes that he "comes to play" and is "great in the clubhouse." If a forty-fifth round draft pick has exactly the same demeanor, no one says anything about it. If a first rounder is animated and fiery while on the mound, he's a "competitor." If a forty-fifth rounder acts exactly the same way, he's a "hothead." If a first rounder talks a lot about hitting with his teammates, he's "trying to learn." If a forty-fifth rounder does the same thing, he's a "clubhouse lawyer." If a first rounder swings big and misses a lot, he's "learning how to hit." If a forty-fifth rounder swings big and misses once in a while, he becomes released. If a first rounder hits .300 with 10 homeruns, he has "tons of potential" and is on a fast track for the big leagues. If a forty-fifth rounder hits .300 with 10 homeruns, he has "maxed out" his potential and often flounders at AA or AAA as an "organizational player." While the "maxing out of potential" in the latter comparison may indeed be true, it doesn't make the pill any less bitter to swallow for the ballplayer involved. If you ever talk to a former minor leaguer who retired at a relatively young age, ask him why. He will probably say, "I got tired of all the BS and politics," or something along those lines. I know he will because every time I met a new teammate, it never failed: he felt the need to tell me how the organization — or several organizations — "shafted" him. The point is that no one, especially the low-round draft pick, wants to see intra-organizational promotions go to players with less impressive numbers. Worse yet, not only does the better-numbers player not receive a promotion, but he often receives his release well before the other guy. Unfortunately, it happens all the time, so consider yourself warned.

You're on your own, kid

In the late 1990s, I remember hearing former Texas A&M football coach R.C. Slocum talk about why a prized recruit chose professional baseball over college football. "With football, there are lots of rules and no money. In baseball, there is lots of money and no rules." I wouldn't say there are "no" rules, but Slocum is pretty close. Basically, no one really cares what you do away from the field. If you don't have to be at the park until 3:30 P.M., then until 3:30 P.M., you can do whatever you want. The same is true for after games. Once you leave the park, you may do as you choose. Want to sleep until 2:30 P.M.? Want to get up at 7:30 A.M. to play with your kids? Want to stay out partying until 4:30 A.M.? Go for it.

In the chapter "The College Experience," I mentioned the "freedom with responsibility" motto that, if not written outright, is implied at colleges and universities worldwide. The same is true in pro baseball. Once you sign a pro contract, regardless of your age, you are expected to be a responsible, professional young man, and part of being responsible and professional is to be on time. Managers don't care if you leave after a game and drive two hours to see someone, but if you have a game the next day, you better be on time. Most managers don't want to hear about car trouble or traffic or oversleeping. If you are late for whatever reason, be a man, accept the punishment (usually a fine), pay it, and don't let it happen again.

It's funny how most managers are very ho-hum about fines. I was late for a bus trip with the High Desert Mavericks in 1997 under manager Chris Speier. We were to leave Bakersfield for San Jose on a Friday morning at 10:00 A.M. As I was inclined to do on a Thursday night during my minor league days, I went out on the town with a couple team-mates to take in the nightlife of Bakersfield. After pouring back a few too many *cervezas* at a Mexican-style bar/club, I stumbled home at about 3:00 A.M. Before we went out that night, my roommate, who did not join us, told me that he would arrange the appropriate wakeup call for the morning, and I trusted him.

The next thing I knew, the phone was ringing at 10:20 A.M. It was our trainer telling my roommate and me that we were late. Obviously, we never got the wakeup call, and since I knew that Speier — with his hardcore, old school mentality — wouldn't want to hear any excuses, I bit my lip and took my medicine. I threw everything into my bag and got to the bus as quickly as possible. Speier, after briefly staring a hole through me with his pale, blue eyes, said, "That's a $25 fine, due by the end of the day." I played in the game that night, went 4–4, and paid my fine, and that was the end of it. No reprimand. No grudges. No sitting on the bench. The next day, it was business as usual between Speier and me.

Incidentally, the punishment system is not always financial. I have a friend who told me that his college coach, apparently unhappy with his team's play during a road trip, made the team do calisthenics and run sprints in the parking lot at 8:00 A.M. The other common type of punishment in the amateur ranks is "benching" a player for on- or off-field transgressions, and anyone who has ever played amateur sports has probably been benched at one time or another. In pro ball, however, a manager rarely benches a player. There are two reasons for this, depending on the type of professional baseball you're playing. In independent leagues, where the emphasis is on winning games and not on player development, if you bench an everyday player, you hurt the team's chances of winning that evening. In affiliated minor league baseball, benching doesn't occur because it could prevent a player from getting his much needed at-bats or innings pitched that evening.

If the punishment system is decidedly "uncollegiate," so is the treatment of the players. During my freshman year of college, I had to give one of our assistant coaches a list of my classes so he could monitor my attendance and progress. When I transferred to Virginia Tech, Coach Phillips met my family and me on campus and spent the entire day driving us around, showing us the sights, and helping me move into my new apartment. Contrast these two events with that of a former teammate of mine, who was a second-round draft pick in the early 1990s.

After receiving and signing his contract, he reported to minicamp, where all the newly signed draft picks report. When he got off the plane, not only was there not a soul there to meet him at the airport, but no one met him at the team hotel, either. When the week-long minicamp broke, he stayed in that same city to play his first professional season, and because no one helped him with finding living accommodations, he ended up spending the remainder of the summer with four other players in a two-bedroom apartment. Nice handling of a raw, intimidated 18-year-old kid, huh?

A lack of quality instruction

You would assume that professional organizations would hire the best, most qualified instructors for their minor league systems, but, lamentably, that's not always the case. For 125 years, baseball has operated in the "good ol' boy" network, wherein jobs are often assigned based on a player's past success on the field and not on his ability to instruct. I have always believed in the quotation, "Those who can, do, and those who cannot, teach." And I also believe this saying transcends sport and cultural barriers. When I was in Australia in November of 1999, I was at Sydney's Olympic Park watching a game between two other countries when I began speaking with an Australian man and his young, baseball-playing son. We talked about a few things, and then he asked me, "Is it the same in America as it is here that the best coaches in sports—not just in baseball—were usually only average players?" Immediately, I answered in the affirmative.

If you think about it, how many Hall of Fame-caliber players have ever gone on to become Hall of Fame-caliber coaches or managers? Very few, and the reason is this: Coaches and managers need to understand the nuances of the game, and, generally, supremely gifted athletes never seem to learn the minutiae of the game. They don't need to. The players of average ability need to gain an edge on the better competition, so they search for ways to maximize their lesser talents. Through this attention to detail, they are better able to understand the game and teach the game to others of average ability. After all, more athletes are "average" rather than exceptional.

My point is that in baseball, it seems as though GM's and Directors often award jobs to former major leaguers because they assume that their ability to reach the big leagues automatically means that they know the game and will therefore become good coaches. Rarely is that the case, especially with hitting coaches. Have you ever heard of Rudy Jaramillo, Rick Down, and Clarence Jones? You'd have to be a baseball junkie to know all of these men, who happen to be among the most highly regarded hitting coaches in baseball. Even the great Charley Lau, whom George Brett credits for his success as a hitter, was only a career .250 hitter at the big league level. Do you think Manny Ramirez, who claims to never look at a pitcher's scouting report before facing him and instead trusts his own instincts, would make a good hitting instructor? Not bloody likely. The late Ted Williams, my baseball hero, said, in *The Science of Hitting*, "Everyone knows how to hit, but few really do." As much as it pains me to disagree with the Splendid Splinter, I think it's the other way: "Everyone hits, but few know how to teach it."

Finally, in 1991, I spent fall break at UNC with a fellow freshman whose father had played in the Minnesota Twins organization in the 1960s. Naturally, since he had done the very thing I wanted to do, I began picking his brain. I asked him about various facets of minor league baseball, and when I got around to asking him about the instruction he received and what he learned, his answer astounded me. He said that while the practice time and number of repetitions were both plentiful, he said that very little teaching occurred and that he didn't learn a whole lot. I couldn't believe that a major league organization (and a top-flight one at that, as the major league-level Twins of the 1960s were a pretty solid team, including a World Series appearance in 1965) didn't provide their future major leaguers with quality instruction. Now, ten years later, having seen minor league baseball from the inside, I can understand why: there simply aren't enough qualified people to teach baseball, and, more specifically, hitting.

The Rovers

During the offseason of 2001–2002, I gave hitting lessons at an indoor batting cage in Santa Rosa, California. Before each lesson with a new hitter (often a 10- to 13-year-old), I would ask him what kind of instruction he had received in the past. The conversation generally would go something like this:

> Has anyone ever told you to hit with your back elbow up?
> Yes.
> Who told you that?
> My dad. (Sometimes, my coach.)
> Did he tell you why you should hit with your back elbow up?

No.
Do you like to hit with your back elbow up?
Not really.
Is it comfortable?
No.
Then don't do it.

Next, I would proceed to another old father's tale — lining up the knuckles.

Has anyone ever told you to line up your knuckles?
Yes.
Who told you that?
My dad. (Sometimes, my coach.)
Did he tell you why you should line up your knuckles?
No.
Show me what that means.

The kid would then grip the bat and line up the big knuckles with the middle knuckles on his hands, or, even worse, the big knuckles with the big knuckles. I would then continue:

Do you like to hit like that?
Not really.
Why not?
It doesn't feel right.

At that point, I would show him how to grip the bat properly, which, incidentally, has nothing to do with knuckles.

My working with these young men confirmed a theory I had postulated ten years ago: It is far better to tell a kid *nothing* about hitting than tell to him something *wrong*. Most kids, if they have any athleticism at all, can figure things out for themselves, and improper coaching detracts from the natural instincts that all good athletes possess. Where am I going with this? Right here.

In all minor league systems, someone carries the title "Pitching Coordinator" and "Hitting Instructor," or something along these lines. There are also organizational infield, outfield, catching, and baserunning instructors. Basically, there is one person in charge of developing a pitching program and theory which all the pitching coaches within the organization must adhere to, and, in turn, teach to their pitchers. The same is true with all the other facets of baseball, too. The general term for these men is the "roving instructor," as they "rove" from minor league town to minor league town within the organization throughout the summer, and baseball players refer to them simply as "rovers."

From what I've seen, the Pitching Coordinator is actually a pretty good idea because it keeps track of "pitch counts," the number of pitches a pitcher throws during an appearance, and prevents a pitcher from overthrowing and potentially damaging his arm. In fact, I know of a minor league manager, who, because of a heated confrontation with a top pitching prospect, left him in a game in which he was getting hit around pretty hard. (Normally, when a pitcher is struggling badly, a manager will remove him from the game so the pitcher can save face.) Well, word got back to the Pitching Coordinator what had happened and that the pitcher had exceeded his strict pitch count by quite a fair margin. In spite of the manager's having led the team to the first-half championship, he was fired shortly thereafter.

When it comes to hitting, though, I've seen rovers do more harm than good. Take the case of Antonio Fernandez. He was a late-round draft pick (50th, I believe) out of the University of New Mexico, chosen by the San Diego Padres. He was a lot like me, actually: not particularly fast, not the greatest body you'd ever want to see, not exactly a rocket launcher from third base but solid defensively, not a power-hitter by any means, but he could flat-out hit the baseball (certainly better than I). I played against Tony in the California League in 1996, and at the All-Star break that year, he was hitting something around .380. Naturally, he was selected to the All-Star team, and though his average tailed off quite a bit over the second half of the season, he still ended up around .330. If you hit .330 in the California League, you had a pretty good year, but, as is often the case in the minor leagues, there were two other third baseman in front of Fernandez whom the organization liked more. The Padres told him that they felt he would never progress within the organization and, therefore, in fairness to Tony, who was a humble, likeable, hard-working guy, wanted to trade him to give him a chance to reach the big leagues.

During the offseason, the Padres traded him to the Milwaukee Brewers, who also had a team in the California League, and in early April of 1997, we faced each other again. It was during a pregame chat wherein I ascertained all of this information. Only six games into the season when we first played, he appeared to be the same, hard-hitting player he was the previous year, but when we played his team again in early June, his average was around the .240 mark. I could see the pain and frustration in his eyes after a tough series against us, a series in which he was hitting the ball but not driving the ball like he had the year before.

Naturally, I had to ask him what the hell was going on at the plate, and he told me that Milwaukee's hitting rover had basically screwed him up something awful. I don't remember exactly what the hitting instructor told him, but the rover's teachings were the opposite of what had worked for Tony during the previous summer. If you hit .330 in the California League, you obviously know how to hit. No, Tony didn't have the jaw-dropping power numbers that a big-time third baseman prospect would have, but he wasn't exactly chopped liver, either. Remember my frustration with the "justification of paycheck" coaches from an earlier chapter? Well, this rover pretty much epitomized one. A good rover would deal with each hitter on a case-by-case basis as opposed to lumping every hitter together and teaching one "style" of hitting. Sometimes—heck, oftentimes—that's just not the case.

One more story regarding rovers. I will acknowledge that I'm an extremely hardheaded and stubborn individual, especially when it comes to theories of hitting, and it didn't take long for my 1996 Visalia teammates to see that. As I mentioned earlier in this chapter, the majority of the team consisted of Detroit Tigers farmhands, and Larry Parrish was the organization's hitting instructor. It was the job of our manager, Tim Torricelli, who doubled as the Oaks hitting coach, to make sure the hitters implemented Parrish's organization-wide theory of hitting. Well, Parrish came to town for the first time in early May, and after listening to my hitting theories for the first month of the season, the guys were anxiously awaiting Parrish's and my first conversation. So, after batting practice one day, during which Parrish stood on the back of the batting cage to monitor his hitters, we retreated to the clubhouse to have our long-awaited hitting discussion. Much to the surprise of my teammates, the chat went quite well; they expected an acid-meets-base kind of reaction.

The point of contention in our theories was, without being too technical, the linear versus rotational styles of hitting. Parrish, who was quite a powerful and successful big league hitter, believed that a hitter should be more linear and focus on shifting weight effectively and getting full extension. I, on the other hand, felt that hitters should track the ball as long as possible before swinging at it and try to hit the ball up the middle and to the opposite field. My theory allows a hitter to follow the pitch for a few more feet and thus to determine what the pitch is before deciding to swing at it; this approach results in far fewer swings at bad pitches and more solid contact. The downside to this approach is that it sacrifices power. Parrish's pet project within the organization was Keith Kimsey, a thin 6'6", 200 lb. outfielder. Keith had a great year from a power standpoint (20 homeruns, I think, in only four months), made the All-Star team, and even received an end-of-season promotion to Class AA. He hit some balls as far as anyone I've ever seen. He also struck out a lot and looked bad in doing so. Comparatively, I hit only four homeruns, but I drove in almost the same numbers of runs, and since I was on base more, I scored more runs.

As a member of the Arizona Diamondbacks, I didn't have to practice Parrish's teachings. In fact, Dwayne Murphy, currently the Diamondbacks' big league hitting coach, was with us from time to time that year. Because there is an unwritten code among co-op teams that one organization's theories should never be taught to another's, Murphy would speak to me—and to the other D'backs hitters—about hitting. The point to this story is that one day late in the season, Torricelli called me into his office to tell me that I was having a nice year and I shouldn't be so vocal about my baseball beliefs in order to avoid stepping on anyone's toes. He knew that I, for the most part, didn't much care for Parrish's theories. He added that whether or not he himself believed in what Parrish was teaching was irrelevant: in the at-times militaristic hierarchy of professional baseball, you—whether you're a manager or a player and whether you agree with them or not—are expected to follow the orders of your superiors. End of story.

Just as I tell the pre-teen boy that not everything a coach or father says is automatically right, the same is true for the professional baseball player when dealing with a rover. In the "dealing with coaches" chapter, I recommended the diplomatic approach of, "Yessir. I'm working on doing it your way." Because the male ego is both pervasive and strong in pro baseball, you may have to adopt the same attitude in order to succeed. For some reason, even before I was around minor league baseball long enough to understand the institution, I sensed a "cow being herded off to slaughter" mentality.

When feeding the cows on our farm, it's amazing how habitual they are. In the summer, when they hear the roaring of the diesel engine in my dad's truck, they know it's feeding time, and they begin their long walk from the pasture to the barn. Once they enter the barn, they know which door will soon be opened to let them into the feeding area, so they wait there for someone to open it. After the door opens, they burst through and charge into the stanchions from which they have been eating every single day for two or three or five or even ten years. When it comes time to ship one off to the slaughterhouse, another young cow takes its place, and for it, the whole process begins anew. Before long, however, the neophyte knows exactly where to go and what to do.

Baseball players don't seem to be much different. God bless 'em, they just aren't among the brightest people in the world. I recently read an interview with the 2000 AL MVP Jason Giambi, who was speaking on his good fortune of being a major leaguer: "It's not like I'm on the Mensa mailing list." That's not a knock against ballplayers. It's just that many of them attend only one or two years of college, or, sometimes, none at all. Others come from countries where education is lacking. Whatever the case, succeeding at baseball is usually more important to a ballplayer than succeeding academically. A trait I have often observed in ballplayers is an almost blind following of authority.

When I became aware of the "cattle" mentality, I vowed I would never become one of the herd. If I were going to end up as ground chuck, I was going to do it *my way*. Early on, I had blindly followed instructions for two simple reasons: (1) I was *so* eager to learn and (2) I simply didn't know any better. I was on the way to my demise when I vowed to myself that from the day I left Chapel Hill, I would never automatically accept the gospel of a coach as the truth. If you've ever seen the bumper sticker "Question Authority," you know what I mean. I never tried to be openly defiant to anyone's instruction, but when I had the least bit of doubt, you can bet the ranch — no pun intended — that I was going to ask some questions. I suggest you do the same. Who wants to end up on someone's dinner plate?

The offseason

I hate to say it, but a lot of times, baseball players choose to hang up their spikes for financial reasons. While such a decision was certainly understandable for a 29-year-old like me, it has to be particularly galling for a 24- or 25-year-old. This book is premised on giving yourself every opportunity to succeed and leaving nothing to chance in your quest for professional baseball. Once you're there, how you spend your offseasons may have a direct impact on your chances of reaching the big leagues.

Unless your signing bonus is quite substantial — if you're reading this book, something tells me that it was not — you will need to have a job during the winter months, unless, of course, you don't have any bills, *i.e.*, rent, car insurance, student loans, etc. Having never lived at home since I left college, I always had bills, so I had to work. For my first pro baseball job, I chose something that I always wanted to do: bartending. Bartending, first of all, fit my lifestyle, as I've always been quite a fan of nightlife. I figured rather than going out and consuming drinks, someone could pay me to mix them. I found bartending, in the right place, to be the most lucrative, short-term job a player can have in the offseason. If you have the right personality makeup and can find the right bar or restaurant or nightclub to be a bartender, I wholeheartedly recommend it.

If you were fortunate enough to earn a bachelor's degree from a four-year college, you may be able to become a substitute teacher. In the state of California, a substitute can make as much as $100 per day, which translates to about $13.50 hour. Not too shabby, huh? It's no secret that many ex-ballplayers become coaches, and becoming a teacher is almost required to coach at the high school level. If you substitute teach in a district in which you plan to coach someday, you will have a chance to develop a rapport with both the kids and the staff, perhaps making yourself more marketable when hiring time comes around.

Also, the day is over at about 3:00 P.M., and there are lesson plans or exams to grade, leaving you plenty of time in the evenings to do your winter workouts. The work itself is not that hard physically — obviously — and at the end of the evening, you shouldn't be too worn out that you might consider skipping your exercises, unlike some jobs. I played with a guy who built fences for an offseason, and he was always talking about how hard the work is. After hearing what he was doing while on the job, I had to agree. Unfortunately for him, he had signed as a junior and never received his bachelor's degree, so while he was stuck lugging around five-gallon buckets of cement all winter long, I was sitting in warm schoolrooms writing books.

On the other hand, there is the menial, thankless job which provides enough motivation to make it to ten big leagues. In one particular offseason, I worked at a truck repair shop. I had looked for a bartending job for about two months, but nothing had presented itself. With bills beginning to pile up and no decent job prospects on the horizon, I accepted an offer from a guy who was a big fan of the baseball team for whom I just played, and knowing that I wanted to stick around for the winter, he told me that he would help me out. I had no choice but to accept. He offered to pay me $8 per hour, which, believe it or not, was more than the going rate for the type of work I was doing. I began working around Halloween and didn't quit until spring training began in late April. I remember spending the days thinking about how miserable I was, how someone with a college degree shouldn't be doing this kind of work. If I had a nickel for every time I thought about going to law school, I'd be a rich man.

After six months of nine-hour days, five days a week, I was sufficiently motivated to have a good year. Furthermore, even though I was usually tired at night when I got home from work, I turned the frustration into motivation when it came to lifting weights at the end of the day. As it turned out, I ended up posting the best numbers of my seven-year pro career. Frustration can be quite the motivator, no?

Outlasting the competition

I can't believe the number of times I've seen a player I played against in my Cal League days who made to the big leagues. Certainly, guys like Eric Chavez and Travis Lee and Miguel Tejada were on the fast track to The Show because of their immense talent, but there several others who made it about whom I could say, "You know, so-and-so was a pretty good ballplayer, but he wasn't *that* much better than I was to make it to the big leagues and I ended up in an independent league."

In a lot of these cases, a player will "be in the right place at the right time," but you won't be in that position if you decided to retire a few months earlier. Believe me, the road to the big leagues is a lot rockier mentally and emotionally than the road to professional baseball, and many a ballplayer has retired because he "got sick and tired of all the BS." I know what you're thinking: "Boy, I would give anything to be able to play minor league baseball, and if I got the chance, I wouldn't just throw it away." Well, have you ever heard the quote, "Don't judge a man until you've walked 1,000 miles in his shoes?" It's easy to sit outside the business of pro baseball and make outrageous claims, but until you've seen what actually goes on within the institution, please do all of us ex-pro ballplayers a favor and bite your tongue.

If ever anyone entered pro baseball as the anti-cynic, it was Gabriel Bo Durkac. In fact, one of the guys in Visalia tabbed me "Just Happy to Be Here" because of my, well, just-happy-to-be-here-and-receiving-a-paycheck-to-play-baseball attitude. Just two years later, when I was in spring training with the Houston Astros, the doubts, the frustration, and the financial instability became too much, and I decided to ask for my release. I didn't know what I wanted to do, but I was no longer happy playing baseball. In less than two years, I went from hopelessly quixotic to hopeless. Baseball — the institution, not the game itself — can do that to you.

The reason I mention this change in attitude is because current major league third baseman Chris Truby was working out with both the Class A and Double A teams in Kissimmee that spring (for the record, he spent more time with the Double A team, but I remember talking to him and fielding ground balls with him at third base). Since he was my competition, I asked a lot of the other players what kind of ability Truby had in order to size up my skills against his. To a man, they said he was outstanding defensively but only a fair hitter. Furthermore, he had been married during that offseason, and coupled with his having spent the six previous years with the Astros in Class A and lower, he seemed ready to move on with his life. In other words, he didn't exactly have the burning desire of a kid right out of high school.

Well, Chris Truby went from being on the fringe of being released in March to the Triple-A World Series in September. Apparently, everything came together for him as a hitter all of a sudden, and hit something crazy like 20 homeruns over the first four months of the Double-A season, which in turn earned him a promotion in August and September. He spent 1999 and 2000 in Triple-A, and he finally got a big league call up at the end of the 2000 season. Then, in 2001, he started the season as the big league team's opening day third baseman. Go figure. It's a simple case of outlasting the competition and being in the right place at the right time.

Going to back to the offseason, think about the financial ramifications of your baseball career. There will undoubtedly come a point when you will look around and say, "Jeez. Look at all my friends. They all have well-paying jobs, houses, families, and are starting put away money for the future." It's only human to compare yourself to them and wonder when the pot of gold at the end of *your* rainbow will appear. But, if you have invested wisely with your signing bonus, received your bachelor's degree, kept your expenses as low as possible, and been lucky enough to find a patient and accommodating employer, you may be able to extend your career a few extra years. Who knows? You might become a Chris Truby.

Professional baseball "ladder"

Major Leagues: American League (15 teams) and National League (15 teams); 162 games

Triple A: International Association (15 teams) and Pacific Coast League (15 teams); 142 games

Double A: Texas League (10 teams), Eastern League (10 teams), and Southern League (10 teams); 142 games

Class A Advanced: California League (10 teams), Carolina League (10 teams), and Florida State League (10 teams); 142 games

Class A: Midwest League (15 teams) and South Atlantic League (15 teams); 142 games

Short-season Class A: New York-Penn League (10 teams) and Northwest League (10 teams); 80 games

Short-season Rookie: Appalachian League (10 teams); 80 games

Rookie: Gulf Coast League (20 teams) and Arizona Summer League (10 teams); 60 games

Glossary

As you've probably noticed, the tone of this book is somewhat serious. I want to impress upon you, the reader, the importance of giving yourself the optimum opportunity to succeed in as a baseball player. Like other phases of the game — hitting, fielding, and strength training, among others — I didn't know much about baseball jargon when I entered college. In this last chapter, I want to have a little bit of fun and give you a head start on baseball lingo.

This glossary originally appeared in my hitting manual and later in an article for BaseballAmerica.com's website. I have included it in order to clarify any terms you may not have totally understood and to introduce you to the terms that ballplayers use. It will allow you to sound like a professional whenever discussing baseball with someone because, after all, if you can't dazzle 'em with brilliance, baffle 'em with BS.

Affiliated baseball: the general term for minor league baseball in which players are under contract with a major league organization

Approach: your own individualized "plan of attack" of hitting

Arm slot: the position of a pitcher's arm at the moment he releases the ball

Arrive on time: the ability to time the reaching of your maximum bat speed with the arrival of the pitch, which is the essence of hitting

Brass: the collective term for the decision-makers within an organization (usually, but not limited to, the General Manager, the Director of Player Development, the Pitching Coordinator, and the Hitting Coordinator)

Breaking ball: the general term for curveballs and sliders

Director of Player Development: the man in charge of all minor league personnel decisions

Dirty/filthy: an adjective used to describe a difficult pitch or pitcher

Drop and drive: a style of pitching in which the pitcher uses the strength of his legs to propel his fastball to home plate; an example would be Tom Seaver

Guessing: looking for a certain pitch or a certain location within the strike zone and not swinging unless the ball is there

Happy zone: a term taken from Ted Williams' *The Science of Hitting*, the part of the strike zone in which an individual hitter handles pitches the best

Head discipline: keeping your head still and down throughout the course of the swing

Hitch: any movement of the hands during the stride

Hitter's count: usually 2–0, 3–0, and 3–1, the counts when getting a fastball is most likely

Hitting deep in the count: putting the ball in play after seeing many pitches in the at-bat

In the bucket: a hitter who steps away from the plate with his stride is said to be stepping "in the bucket"

Independent league: a league in which the players are not under contract with a major league organization

Justification of paycheck coach: any coach who, because he is being paid to coach hitting, gives a lot of unnecessary and oftentimes improper advice

Leaking: any positive movement — usually of the feet, hips, or shoulders — that occurs before the decision to swing is made; can severely hinder a player's ability to generate bat speed

Linear: a style of hitting that emphasizes a strong weight shift to supply bat speed

Mistake: any pitch that doesn't go where the pitcher wanted it to go; most mistakes end up over the heart of the plate

On the black: a pitch that just touches that outside or inside corner of the plate is said to be "on the black"

Offspeed pitch: any non-fastball thrown by the pitcher

Paint: to throw a pitch on the corner; "he painted the outside corner with that fastball"

Pitch count: the number of pitches a pitcher throws in an outing

Pitcher's pitch: a pitch that is a strike on the extreme outer edge of the strike zone; usually very difficult to hit solidly

Power position: the ideal body position of a hitter at the point of contact

Rotation: the turning of the hips that, along with a good weight transfer, creates the bat speed that the hitter generates

Rover: a slang term for an organization's roving instructor because he roams from minor town to minor league town to work with players; most organizations have pitching, catching, hitting, and baserunning "rovers"

Runs produced: RBI's + runs scored − homeruns. Most baseball people consider this most important stat because it translates directly into what you are doing to help your team win

Spit on: to take a pitch, usually a very close one

Step in the bucket: striding away from the plate; lefties striding toward 1st base and righties toward 3rd base

Study hall: a program found in almost all colleges and universities that requires certain student-athletes to spend time studying among academic coordinators and tutors

Sweet spot: the part of the bat and ball that is the hardest

Taking: not swinging at a pitch

Tall and fall: a style of pitching in which the pitcher uses his height and leverage to propel his fastball towards home plate; this technique also creates a downward plane on the pitch, making it difficult for the batter to elevate the ball; an example would be Randy Johnson

Tool: a term used by scouts to evaluate the natural ability of ballplayers; some common tools are running speed, arm strength, and fastball velocity

Triple Crown: leading the league in RBI's, homeruns and batting average

Walk on: a student who attempts to try-out and make a collegiate team; sometimes the coaches might have seen him play previously, and other times they might not have seen him play

Weight shift: the transfer of the body's weight from the back side to the front side during the course of the swing

Working the count: taking a lot of pitches in at-bat until you get one you like

Index